Life
Coaching

D0877446

Life
Coaching
Change your life in
7 days

EILEEN MULLIGAN

piatkus

PIATKUS

First published in Great Britain in 1999 by Piatkus Books Ltd
This paperback edition published in 2011 by Piatkus

A CIP catalogue record for this book
is available from the British Library.

ISBN 978-0-7499-4190-1

The author and publisher would like to thank Andrew Leigh and
Century Business Books for their permission to use the extract from
The Perfect Decision on pages 82–4 of this book.

Typeset by Phoenix Photosetting, Chatham, Kent
Printed and bound in Great Britain by
Clays Ltd, St Ives plc

Papers used by Piatkus are from well-managed forests
and other responsible sources.

MIX
Paper from
responsible sources
FSC® C104740

Piatkus
An imprint of
Little, Brown Book Group
100 Victoria Embankment
London EC4Y 0DY

An Hachette UK Company
www.hachette.co.uk

www.piatkus.co.uk

Contents

Acknowledgements

With sincerest thanks to all my clients whose contribution made this book possible.

I would also like to thank Andrew Walton, Andrew Leigh and Mark Ellis. Special thanks go to Alex Games for his help in writing this book.

Introduction

Dear Eileen

I am writing to thank you for the dramatic changes you enabled me to bring to my life. I still can't believe how different this year has been from last year. It's not as if life is suddenly problem-free, but since I set out on your coaching programme, I have come to appreciate how important it is to have balance in my life.

For many years I had been trying to change my old ways, but it seemed impossible. Whenever a new obstacle arose, I simply ducked out of the way of confronting it, or told myself that if I ignored it it might go away. I had goals, of course, but they seemed out of reach.

With your help I am happy to say that I can concentrate on finding a solution and not losing sight of my goals. I use the techniques you taught me every day and now have the confidence to face new challenges.

Above all else, I want to thank you for giving me the much needed push to take responsibility for my life, and to find the necessary control that always seemed lacking. I can think of a great many people who would benefit from having you as their coach, so please give some thought to my suggestion of writing a book.

Yours sincerely
Margaret B

That letter is one of many I've received from satisfied clients. I chose to reproduce it here not just because I'm proud of it (which

I am!) but because it came at a very important moment in the development of my new business. I had just taken the risky decision to go solo; to do one-to-one personal coaching. Even though I was sure I was doing the right thing, I was still nervous, and positive feedback from clients was just the sort of response I needed to validate my work.

You see, many people want to change, but feel prevented from doing so, sometimes by circumstances that seem beyond their control. This can be enormously frustrating, and it weighs on the mind. That letter is an example of how liberating it feels when you are finally able to say to yourself: now I can move on. That's a feeling I want you to experience, because I know the difference it made to my life.

I'm a personal coach. Coaching is an American phenomenon but it's rapidly gaining popularity in the UK and around the world. The way it works is that the coach usually works with you over the telephone, after an initial face-to-face session, to help you sort out your personal and professional problems. The new generation of coach is not just concerned with physical well-being. They work on your professional career, finances, spiritual growth, relationships – even your social life. They are there to push you to change your life for the better. I speak from experience here, because coaching certainly changed my own life.

A few years ago, I lay virtually paralysed for two months until spinal surgery finally put me back on my feet. It was a turning point for me, because my life had been monumentally out of balance until then. With a new year approaching, I decided this was the opportunity I needed to get myself in order. 'OK,' I said to myself, 'you have one week to change your life: how would you do it?' Each day I reviewed a different area of my life, and identified seven major areas that became the foundation of my coaching programme.

1. **Health** This is an obvious place to start. By conditioning your body and mind you will get the best from them and be able to use them to their full potential. I will show you how to assess your health and incorporate minor changes into your lifestyle to help you to achieve major results.

Practical advice will help you to achieve a fitter and healthier body. I also look at the significance of prevention rather than cure, the importance of relaxation and avoiding sickness as the 'easy option'. There are also methods for improving your mental and physical stamina to enable you to achieve your goals.

2. **Spiritual/religious life** Spiritual and religious beliefs are central to many people's value systems, and I will help you to see the connection, and how it influences your coaching programme. It enables you to affirm your sense of purpose and recognising that you are not just a physical and emotional being but a person with genuine spiritual needs too. I will show you how you can pursue a spiritual life without abandoning your commercial goals. Also, what to do if there is conflict between your goals and spiritual beliefs, and when you might find it useful to contribute to this area.

3. **Work and career** Assessing your current job – why do you do what you do, and does it provide you with everything you want? What do you really want to do? What choices do you have? I will show you how to get the career you desire, identify what is important to you, set the right goals for yourself, improve your development skills and deal with work-related problems.

4. **Finances** How much money is enough, and why do even high earners have sleepless nights worrying about money? You will find out how to establish your value, take control of your finances, practical budgeting, and how to set goals and achieve results in this area.

5. **Personal relationships** What do you want from your relationship? Techniques for bringing the right relationship into your life, and knowing when to move away from the wrong one. Know your own goals before trying to pursue joint goals in a relationship. How not to be afraid to ask for what you want. Dealing with your emotions, and having the courage to make the right decision for you.

6. **Family/extended family** How to get on with those people whom fate, not friendship, chose for you. Improving family bonds, and setting clear boundaries. Dealing with family rifts, and moving through old issues that previously kept you blocked.

7. **Friends/social life** Would you want to change your friends? Would you want them to change you? Some friends have a vested interest in keeping you where you are. This is about how to recognise which friends are helping you to move forward – as opposed to holding you back. Finding your coaching buddies, and getting the best from your social life.

This programme will reveal exactly what it is you need to turn yourself into your own coach. It is tailor-made to suit you, and once you see the difference coaching can make to you, you will understand why I say that the seven steps are a way of life, not just for today or the next seven days but for the rest of your life.

For me, the seven steps also opened the door to a new career which is vastly different from what I was doing before. After starting out in the nursing profession, I later trained as a beauty therapist before founding an international beauty company. In 1995 I was Cosmopolitan Entrepreneur of the Year, and I was given a Gucci/Business Age award as one of the forty most exciting young entrepreneurs in Britain. As a result of this, Carlton TV featured me in their documentary about self-made millionaires.

But behind the scenes it was a very different story. A personal relationship had gone to the wall, complicated by the fact that the man involved was also my business partner. Subsequent board-room struggles sent me reeling. In the circumstances, something had to give, and it did – my back. I didn't want to be just another casualty of executive stress, so I determined to coach myself out of this crisis.

Being, quite literally, stopped in my tracks allowed me to make the changes I needed to get my life back in order. Balance was the key and this is the foundation to the coaching programme you are about to enter.

Instead of focusing on one area of my life as I had always done before – work and career – I now realised the relevance of success in every area and the consequences of ignoring that. Success is often determined by its trappings: disposable income, big house, designer clothes. While success is a worthy goal, you need to question what it means to you so that you can experience it on a personal level.

I felt that, with my business experience and my contacts, coaching was a good area to move into. A lot of friends and business colleagues backed me up. The first couple of months were like walking a tightrope but I had the confidence to go on because I was sure I would succeed. Also, I had plenty of contacts and goodwill from my former clients. I'm glad to say it worked, and pretty soon I had a client list that ranged from Members of Parliament, housewives and business executives to celebrities and lawyers.

▪ Coaching Yourself

Since you've made the decision to pick up this book, I'm gambling that there's some area of your life marked 'Could Do Better'. It may be an aspect of your business life that's troubling you: are you finding decision making a problem? Or maybe you're concerned about work problems, but not sure how to go about getting the best out of yourself or other people.

Or, perhaps it's your personal life. It could be that you don't feel as fit as you'd like to be (maybe you want to give up smoking) or you're finding it difficult to get out of bed in the morning, or your confidence is not what it should be. Relationship problems, concerns over moving home ... I could go on! Whatever the problem, by picking up this book, you've signalled to yourself that you want to sort things out, and I'm very glad you have done.

In this book I'm going to show you how to be your own coach. The book is divided into two main areas. Part 1 is a preparation for the Seven Steps that comprise Part 2. In it, you will develop new skills that allow you to realise your value, work through problems with a positive focus, eliminate the excuses, do away with negative behaviour patterns and create the space you need to make changes. I'm going to describe the tools you need before you begin, as well as the forms that you will be filling in as you work through the book.

The forms which you will find in Part 4 are exactly the same forms that I use to work with clients when I do one-to-one coaching sessions with them. As you work through Part 1, you will look at how you can get in touch with your Values and how to set Goals that are appropriate to you. You will work on Developing a Positive Mental Attitude, as well as techniques for policing your own thoughts, building self-esteem and overcoming fear. I will talk about creating a Happy Space and describe the Problem-Solving Zone. I will look at Time Management, and ask why your life is the way it is, and who or what do you blame. The final chapter in Part 1 is called Communication Skills. It shows you how to use compromise to your advantage, and how it helps to listen if you want to be heard. There will be exercises in each chapter to drive these points home.

Part 2 describes the Seven Steps to changing your life. You can take these a day at a time, or you can take as long as you want to work out each step. After all, this coaching programme is for life. What's crucial is that you absorb the lessons from each step before moving on. Seven Days to Change Your Life. Can it be done? In short, yes. Good luck!

PART 1

Being Your Own
Coach

CHAPTER ONE

The Coaching Process

M Y AIM IN WRITING this book is to translate the simple yet powerful methods I use during my life-coaching sessions with clients. And, as I tell my clients, the object of life coaching is to find exactly what you need to move forward and achieve your goals, and always be prepared to work hard to get it. So what will life coaching do for you? How about this list: Reassess your life, redefine success, set new goals, overcome problems and challenges, change lifelong habits, build confidence and self-esteem. Sounds too good to be true? Now go and look at yourself in a mirror. See that person there? You're looking at your brand new personal coach!

When you think of a coach, what do you think of? A fitness trainer, perhaps: someone who gets you out of bed early one day in the middle of winter and marches you up and down the park doing bending and stretching exercises? Or perhaps you had in mind a language coach, who devises a plan tailor-made to get you from zero to basic French just in time for your holiday in the south of France? In both cases, the one-to-one approach succeeds because your coach works out where you need to focus. If you were in a class of thirty people, a lot of the teacher's time would be wasted by having to attend to everyone's different strengths and weaknesses. That's the beauty of individual coaching: less waste, more haste.

These days, when time is so precious that we feel we cannot afford to waste a moment, more and more people are turning to coaches. And of course the principles of coaching are being explored in other areas. Some of you may have heard about executive coaches or personal mentors, and you can buy cassettes which will promise you the world in the time it takes to listen to a couple of tapes, but I had never seen a coaching book that was relevant to the work I was doing.

A coach is like a best friend. Your coach is there to rejoice in your triumphs, support you through difficult times and help you get the best from yourself. In fact, even though we may not be aware of it, we have all performed the role of coach at times, as well as benefiting from being coached. Spend a few moments to reflect on the times you have:

► offered support

► accepted support

► asked someone a difficult and revealing question

► been asked a difficult and revealing question

► taught someone a new skill

► learnt a new skill

► rejoiced in the triumph of achieving a goal

► could see the solution to a problem, when others could not

► had no solution to a problem, when others had.

This book will be your daily textbook. This is an interactive programme that requires constant input. I strongly suggest you work through each chapter in the order presented. You may find it hard work, but I promise you will get more out of it that way. Don't believe me? I guarantee that, as you work through the targeted questionnaires, checklists and action plans, as well as study the inspiring case histories, you'll see for yourself how coaching gets results.

▪ Preparation

Before you begin, I'd like you to get hold of the following:

An A4 pad You can use your pad for compiling your coaching forms, and, when necessary, adding to them.

A large journal or diary There are various exercises to complete where you will be asked to list feelings, emotions, thoughts and plan strategies.

An A4 folder As you will be reorganising your life, it's important that you keep your forms together, and that everything is on hand for easy reference. The folder will also include any relevant information you gather along the way. You might read an article in a newspaper about a healthy eating plan, for example, and decide to cut it out and stick it in your folder.

Scissors and glue These will come in handy for cutting out any relevant articles you come across and sticking them in your folder.

A selection of coloured pens or crayons These are useful for highlighting important points. Life is never black and white, and that's why I recommend adding plenty of colour and variety to your coaching programme.

This list is important. Why? Because you want your life to be exciting and colourful, don't you? You may have a very strong mental image of the sort of goals you want to achieve, and having a visual image can help to bring the overall picture even closer. You can fill your folder with information that will not only increase your self-knowledge but also give you a greater awareness of the goals you are pursuing. As you go through this book, you will be given techniques to expand your capacity to dream and visualise. Incorporating these techniques into your folder is the first step to realising your goals.

▪ How Do You Feel

As you start the coaching process, I'd like you to fill in the short life chart below which states exactly how you're feeling right now. As you can see, it covers the seven areas of your life that I mentioned in the Introduction. This is base camp: the point from which you will set out. Give yourself a score for each of these areas. If you're really miserable or discontented, give yourself a 1. If you couldn't be happier, put a score which reflects that. I imagine most of you will be somewhere within those two extremes, which is fine: just put a ring round the score that best reflects your initial feelings. We'll come back to it later as we go through the book.

	Low									*High*
▪ Health	1	2	3	4	5	6	7	8	9	10
▪ Spiritual/religious life	1	2	3	4	5	6	7	8	9	10
▪ Work/career	1	2	3	4	5	6	7	8	9	10
▪ Financial	1	2	3	4	5	6	7	8	9	10
▪ Personal relationships	1	2	3	4	5	6	7	8	9	10
▪ Family/extended family	1	2	3	4	5	6	7	8	9	10
▪ Friends/social life	1	2	3	4	5	6	7	8	9	10

How was that? Not too difficult I hope. It's always a good idea to give yourself a score at the beginning of any coaching programme. It establishes where you are, and it's essential for you to have something to compare with later on.

There are also seven separate forms included with the coaching programme – one for each of the areas listed above. As I said in the Introduction, these forms are central to my coaching method, and are exactly the same ones that I use when I'm working one-to-one with clients. When you have completed this chapter, I'd like you to fill in the seven forms that you will find at the back of the book to give yourself a more precise idea of how you feel you're doing in each area of your life. You may find it easier to copy them out on to your A4 pad, rather than use the forms reproduced here. But first, let's take a few minutes to go through exactly how you should fill them in, using the sample form below as a guide.

HEALTH

Goals

1

2

3

Personal Strengths

1

2

3

Immediate Challenges/Blocks/Problems

1

2

3

Development Skills

1

2

3

Achievements

1

2

3

Goals

Make sure your goals are positive and about things you want in your life, not about things you want to eliminate. One client of mine started by writing: 'I want to feel less tired when I wake up.' Can you see how that gets off on the wrong foot? When you express yourself in such a negative way, you're not setting yourself a goal, you're describing a problem. After some discussions she changed her goal so that it read: 'I want to wake up feeling full of energy.' It was a subtle but important choice of words, and one that reflected a change of attitude: Goals are things that you want to get out of life, not a life that you want to get out of.

Here are some examples of goals for each of the seven steps:

1. **Health:** To get fit.

2. **Spiritual/religious life:** To go to church every Sunday.

3. **Work/career:** To get a promotion in the next three months.

4. **Financial:** To save 10 per cent of my salary each month.

5. **Personal relationships:** To spend more time with my partner.

6. **Family/extended family:** To visit my family more often.

7. **Friends/social life:** To get together with my friends more often.

Personal Strengths

Look for your strengths, not your weaknesses. These can include anything from having a good fitness level and being committed to getting in shape or, in relation to some of the other areas, being supportive, understanding, good at your job, flexible, patient, having a pension plan – the list is endless. Again, don't negate any of your strengths. A client of mine once wrote: 'I appear assertive, although I'm not.' I had to say to him: 'Stop when you get to "assertive"!' That last qualifying phrase was undercutting the strength he needed to draw on. Throw it out! It will only hold you back.

Let's look at some more personal strengths, working through the seven steps.

1. **Health:** I have just received the all-clear after my medical check-up.

2. **Spiritual/religious life:** I find great comfort in my spiritual beliefs.

3. **Work/career:** I received a glowing appraisal from the personnel department.

4. **Financial:** I have never had an overdraft in my life.

5. **Personal relationships:** I have a loving and happy relationship.

6. **Family/extended family:** I love the company of my family.

7. **Friends/social life:** I always make an effort to be there for my friends.

Immediate Challenges/Blocks/Problems

This is where you should list the negative things, but keep your focus on problems that directly affect you. Listing problems that blame or involve other people will keep you blocked. Be careful not to say: 'I work long hours and don't have time to exercise.' Recognise it's up to you to make time. Not exercising is the problem in the Health category, not your long working hours. To give another example in your Work area, if you wrote: 'Clients seem to treat my colleagues well and me badly', you're identifying a negative aspect of a client's behaviour instead of focusing on your own problem which relates to your inability to communicate with your client. We'll be going into this in more depth later on. Finding the cause will lead to the solution.

1. **Health:** I have many sleepless nights because I am very stressed.

2. **Spiritual/religious life:** I am unclear what my own beliefs are because my parents imposed their beliefs on me.

3. **Work/career:** I find my job boring and unfulfilling.

4. **Financial:** I am always spending beyond my means.

5. **Personal relationships:** I struggle to communicate my needs to my partner.

6. **Family/extended family:** I regularly have arguments with my teenage daughter.

7. **Friends/social life:** I allow my friends to dictate my social life.

Development Skills

You can increase development skills in every area of your life. In your Health area, joining a gym or reading a book on nutrition will aid your development. In areas like Work and Career, qualifications and training courses are all relevant skills. That may be less obvious in the area of Personal Relationships, but what about improving your communication skills or learning to be a better listener? The development skills you set have to be relevant to your goals, so if your goal is to run a marathon and you're starting from scratch, the first thing you may need is information about the venue, the level of fitness required and having a fitness assessment before you start running five miles before breakfast each morning. When you set goals, you don't plan to fail, so make sure you don't fail to plan.

1. **Health:** Learn to swim.

2. **Spiritual/religious life:** Take up meditation.

3. **Work/career:** Enrol on the management training programme.

4. **Financial:** Stay within my monthly budget.

5. **Personal relationships:** Learn to listen to my partner.

6. **Family/extended family:** Not to get pulled into family disputes.

7. **Friends/social life:** Be less concerned with what my friends think of me.

Achievements

List achievements you are proud of. You'd certainly be proud if you'd run that marathon! Another client of mine who was in an unsatisfactory personal relationship said, 'Well, I've stuck it out for two years.' Some time later, that relationship ended, but I persuaded her to change her comments to: 'I've shown that I can commit to a relationship.' She now had an achievement that was positive even if the relationship was not. Some people can make their achievements sound like personal failures! That's not what this book is about.

1. **Health:** I visit the gym every week.

2. **Spiritual/religious life:** I am no longer afraid to look at this area.

3. **Work/career:** I have the best attendance record in the company.

4. **Financial:** I have saved up enough for an annual holiday.

5. **Personal relationships:** I have been happily married for twenty years.

6. **Family/extended family:** I have three beautiful children.

7. **Friends/social life:** I have stayed in contact with all my old school friends.

▪ The Forms

Now it's time to fill in the forms that you will be using throughout this book. The reason I say 'fill in' rather than 'complete' is that your forms will change constantly as you progress through each chapter. The chapters are designed to prompt you to review your goals and evaluate the information you have put on your forms. It will become apparent when you need to change goals or set ones that are more appropriate to your life. As you change, so will your forms. If you were not able to realise your goals in the past, all that is about to change.

If you can, choose a time of day to complete them when you are at your most relaxed, such as at the end of the day. I normally tell clients to change into casual clothes and put on some soothing music but it's up to you: whatever helps you to concentrate, just do it. When you have completed the forms, lay them out in front of you side by side. Look at your life chart, the chart you filled in earlier with scores from 1 to 10. Spend a few minutes reviewing the chart and forms, and make any alterations you feel are necessary.

CHECKLIST

✔ A4 pad:

✔ Large journal or diary

✔ A4 folder:

✔ Scissors and glue

✔ Selection of coloured pens or crayons

▪ Conclusion

▶ Make sure you have everything on the checklist.

▶ Try and read each chapter in order. Ask yourself if you are committed to your coaching programme. (The correct answer is 'Yes'!)

▶ Have you completed the forms? Do you have everything you need to progress?

▶ Be honest in your answers: always attempt an answer, even when you're not sure. The forms are very revealing, so if your feathers have been ruffled, take heart – you're on the way to making changes.

CHAPTER TWO

Values and Goals

NOW THAT YOU HAVE completed your forms, you're ready to get going. If you have had problems doing so, it may be because you're not clear about your values, or haven't prioritised them.

Everything you hold dear to you and fight to preserve stems from your own personal value system. Imagine life without integrity or a code of conduct for human behaviour. It hardly bears thinking about. Yet, all the same, how clear are you when it comes to your own value system? Let's find out, by looking at a case of conflicting values.

A friend of mine once witnessed a work colleague fiddle her expense sheet. She told her that if it happened again, she would have to report it. After all, my friend was responsible for signing off the expenses. Was she thanked for her warning? You bet she wasn't. In fact a full-scale lecture followed which lasted for nearly an hour, all about how the company was making such high profits, they could afford it, it wasn't if they paid decent wages etc. It was clear that the warning would be ignored. This caused my friend a real dilemma. Stealing from a company is a sackable offence, not an easy one to have on your conscience. However, keeping quiet felt like colluding in the crime.

What would you have done? There is no simple solution, and the right decision is not always the easiest, but if you can fall back upon your true values, that will make it easier to live with your decision. When you struggle to make decisions there is either a conflict taking place with your values or a lack of clarity as to what they are, so let's look at establishing your core values, or reminding yourself of what they are.

▪ Finding a Value

The values referred to in this chapter are life values, or what I term core values. Each value you list may have a subsidiary value that branches off it. For example, you may list security as a major value, which could branch off into financial or emotional security, but to begin with, make a list of your ten most important core values. If you come up with more than ten values, feel free to add them to your list. It's important that you write down everything significant to your life.

It may help you to read through some common values my clients list:

Love	Marriage	Respect
Security	Power	Achievements
Health	Passion	Acceptance
Happiness	Integrity	Humour
Money	Success	Kindness
Adventure	Freedom	Independence
Travel	Understanding	Excitement
Honesty	Compassion	Intimacy
Children	Trust	

Now that you've familiarised yourself with your core values, let's go back to my friend and her dilemma with the expense forms. Here's what she did, after we had talked it through.

'I wish I had never seen her do it,' she said to me. 'At least then I'd be none the wiser'. That set me thinking. It sounded like it was pretty easy to fiddle those expense sheets. Unless someone saw you do it, the chances were it would go unnoticed. My friend was alarmed to hear this, but soon saw what I was getting at. Maybe the problem lay with the expense forms themselves. It was certainly easier to tackle this one than risk being ostracised by other work colleagues. So, that's what she did. Not only were the new forms much more fool-proof; they also required a declaration of honesty from the claimant.

You can hit a wall when you see your problems in black and white, because the solutions in front of you appear so extreme. Keep your value in mind and focus on other ways to find a solution, which will satisfy your value. A bit of lateral thinking is sometimes required. Talk it over with a friend. They are not caught up in the emotional issue and can often see the middle ground.

▪ Prioritising Your Values

Having your values in place is the starting point. What you need to do now is place them in order of importance. This will help you to prioritise your goals and get to work immediately on what you need to bring into your life.

Take a look at the list below:

1. Success	**6.** Ambition
2. Achievements	**7.** Contribution
3. Independence	**8.** Happiness
4. Money	**9.** Health
5. Career	**10.** Love

Have you guessed who wrote that list? Yes, it was me. It's hardly surprising with happiness, love and health so far down the list that my life was once lacking in these areas. The old values I had are common to a lot of people and while they are not necessarily wrong values, they weren't right for me. The goals I set were based around the top priority values, which only reflected one area of my life – work. In my experience you can achieve any goal you put your mind to. But what happens when you get what you think you want and your life still feels incomplete? How do you give back the toy after kicking up such a storm to get it? The answer lies in how you prioritise values and set goals around them.

When you prioritise your values, think long and hard about them. I say this because I made the mistake of thinking that my values needed a certain running order to achieve my business goals. In the process I earned myself a reputation of being cold and hard. It was neither a desired nor rewarding persona to take on. However, all mistakes can be converted to useful lessons. It's OK to get it wrong. In fact, when you do, you are much more likely to get it right the next time. If you thought defining values was easy, think again. Often, realising a true value and living up to it means letting go of an old way of life and making way for the new. If you find this a scary thought, I'm with you a hundred per cent of the way.

▪ Interpreting Your Values

Before, I had success on the top of my list, which at the time only related to my work. It could have been interpreted as having a successful relationship, or enjoying good health. By seeing how values fitted in to every area of my life, health became a top priority value because without that, everything on my old list fell by the wayside.

Here is my new list, together with how I interpreted each value.

- Health – mental, physical and spiritual
- Love – to love and be loved
- Happiness
- Contribution and balance
- Security – financial, emotional
- Personal growth
- Integrity, honesty, sincerity and loyalty
- Understanding, change, variety and new challenges
- Achievements
- Humour

Spend a few minutes interpreting your chosen values and what they mean to you. For example, if you list security, what would it take to make you feel secure? Money, love or perhaps a pension plan? If you list happiness, what would it take to make you happy? Winning the lottery, or having children? You need to be sure that the goals you are pursuing will bring about the results you desire.

▪ Setting Goals That Are Appropriate To Your Value System

Successful people set goals. That sounds simple enough: set yourself a few goals and you're on your way, but let's not overlook the obstacles you will face. To overcome them and remain intact, goals have to be part of your personal growth and value system. If they are not, you can get there by blind determination, but don't expect to arrive intact at the end.

So far, you've listed your core values and prioritised your most important values, and you know what each means to you. Now it should be a lot easier to set goals that are appropriate to your value system, so if you want to review some of the goals you have already set for yourself, look at them in conjunction with your values. So, for example, if making money is an important goal on your Finance chart, you would expect to see it included in your values.

Howard should have been happy with his lot, but nevertheless seemed unable to enjoy his affluent lifestyle. Howard compared his successful company, flash motor, HDP (Highly Desirable Property), luxury holidays and so on against his problems which he recited like a shopping list: 'There's the wife – the less said about her the better; the two kids – bone idle; the ex-wife from hell; the pending law suit; the interest rates; the unfinished extension . . .' At times, it almost seemed like Howard was competitive about his problems. When I put this question to him he burst out: 'It's hardly surprising, with all the problems I've got.' At that time, Howard was convinced he had more problems than anybody else. The turning point came when we discussed the issue of values. When Howard started to define his true values, they had little to do with the trappings of wealth he had listed. As he got more in touch with his values, he said: 'It never occurred to me that I had been collecting

straw trophies. Over the years I've lost sight of what's really important in my life.'

Of course the problem with 'straw trophies' is that they carry no
weight. If you put them on a scale with problems, the balance will
never be tilted in your favour. We often assume certain things will
make us happy, but when they don't you have to find a reason
why. Problems can seem like the obvious answer. In the case of
Howard, he had been weighing up his problems alongside what
was good in his life, or what he thought was good. As he began to
explore and define his true value system, he looked at his forms
again and realised that his original goals focused on his achieving
greater material success, and that this was unimportant to him.
His new goals related to his true core value system, namely to have
a more successful family life, and to tackle his problems rather
than sticking them in a trophy cupboard.

None of us likes to admit we got it wrong but we all do. In fact,
it's OK to admit you got it wrong and don't know what you want.
I'm not suggesting you should protest your problems all the time.
Once you admit you don't know what you want, you've taken the
first step towards focusing on what you do want.

Going back to the drawing board is a scary experience, but it
will serve to put you back in touch with your true values. There
lies the key to discovering not only what you want, but also and
more importantly, what you need.

▪ Reconsidering Your Goals

This may be a good time to look at your goals again and see how
they weigh up against your values. It's worth while being aware of
the consequences that arise from ignoring or overriding them.
There is little to be gained from achieving goals that are not preceded by values.

Melanie had a high-flying career in the city, which was now threatened by a crisis of confidence. Four out of the seven areas of her
coaching chart scored between 8s and 9s. In stark contrast her
work/career scored a 4, as did her relationship chart. Melanie's

spiritual/religious form, which is optional to clients, was not completed. It can be coincidental that two areas match with an exact low score. But based on the contrast with the rest of her chart, I was not surprised to learn that Melanie had been involved in a relationship with her boss for two years. Melanie's major concern at the initial consultation was that she felt undermined by the relationship and her self-esteem was very low.

Her boss spent at least four nights a week with Melanie. At weekends he returned to his wife and three children. His wife was apparently unaware of the affair, and Melanie had made a point of informing me that she had no problem having a relationship with a married man. Maybe she thought her coach would disapprove, but I told her that a personal coach is not there to act as a moral judge or to impose their own value system.

I encouraged Melanie to talk about her goals for a personal relationship. She spoke about having a loving and supportive partner, getting married before she was thirty and a desire to have children. I asked if Melanie had her present partner in mind for a future husband. 'No,' she said, 'I don't want to feel responsible for taking him away from his wife and children. Anyway, I would prefer someone who hasn't been married before.'

I asked her if she would tolerate her future husband having an affair. Her reaction was one of outrage at the thought of such a thing happening. She spoke about the importance of trust, loyalty and fidelity in marriage, then paused and said, 'You must think I'm such a hypocrite...'. 'Why would I think that?' I replied.

Melanie then opened up, not only to me, but also more importantly to herself. She was overwhelmed by guilt, and her family who were Catholic, all disapproved of the relationship. She was also out of touch with her faith. Deep down Melanie felt that the affair was wrong. Her low self-esteem and the feeling of being undermined had more to do with the corrosive damage guilt causes than the behaviour of her partner. Although Melanie did not seek marriage from him, there was clearly a deep physical and emotional attraction that resulted in her overriding her personal values. Now that she had reaffirmed those values it was obvious that a painful decision lay ahead. She knew she had to end the relationship because not only was it conflicting with her values, it was also standing in the way of her goals. At the start of Melanie's coaching, although she was clear about her problems she wasn't clear about the causes. Coaching Melanie to look at her values allowed her to see that her problems were symptoms of a deeper problem: a conflict of values. Making a painful decision paved the way to Melanie finding a new job and a happy relationship.

CHECKLIST

✔ Have you got your value system in place before pursuing a goal?

✔ Ask yourself: 'What is it I want and why do I want it?'

✔ Are you prepared to live up to your values?

✔ What changes are needed in your life to get you back on track?

✔ Don't ignore your values – they won't go away.

✔ List your values at the front of your folder and refer to them daily

As always, be honest with yourself. Your personal success depends on it.

▪ Conflicting Values

Conflicting values occur for numerous reasons. They may be due to religious beliefs, parental values, politics, cultural differences and even love. Following a path mapped out by others can have a certain comfort factor to it. You'll be unlikely to get lost along the way. And the chances are there will be plenty of people to keep you company on your journey. But will you reach your desired destination? You know the feeling you get when you are somewhere you don't want to be. No matter how comfortable the surroundings are, you feel out of place – like you don't fit in.

Coming to terms with your own values is like finding a comfortable pair of old shoes. Walking is a whole lot easier, plus you get further. Taking on other people's values is like squeezing your foot in the wrong shoe. It might look smart to begin with, but the problem is it doesn't fit. And no amount of pushing or shoving will make it fit.

So why would we want to take on other people's values in the first place? It might be a means to get what they've got, or to gain approval. Well even if you get it, chances are you'll come limping past the finishing post. After all, you started off with a disadvantage. What about getting approval? That's a tricky one. I've yet to meet anyone who is not concerned about gaining approval. You may not seek the approval of the masses, but what about those you love and care about? Would you willingly seek the disapproval of a parent, partner, your children or a close friend? Of course not.

I remember my four-year-old niece protesting that a new jacket bought for her birthday didn't fit. As it clearly did fit on the outside, her mother made her wear it, until it became obvious that the sulky-faced child would continue to protest. Finally her mother gave in and my niece flung off the jacket, giving it a kick for good measure. And the moral of that story? What fits on the outside may not fit on the inside.

It may not always be appropriate or even safe to please yourself. There is room for compromise in many situations. At the risk of offending or hurting feelings you can often contend with boring parties, wearing an unfortunate Christmas purchase, visiting the in-laws or munching your way through a tasteless meal, without experiencing a major value conflict. Even then you may need to draw the line, however. It's fine when your values are respected. The problem arises when the line you draw becomes the dividing line.

It can result in you being shunned by friends and family, ridiculed, disowned and isolated from loved ones. The important question you are then faced with is: what is more important – having approval or living up to a value? This question becomes more difficult when you can't have both: there's an easier decision and there's the right decision. The decision you make has to be right for you.

Sanjay moved to England from India with his parents when he was five years old. Much of his extended family lived in England and he had a close bond with them, but he came to me because he wanted his parents to stop interfering in his personal life. Sanjay had scored highly in every area of his life chart apart from personal relationships. Much to his horror, his parents were in the process of selecting an appropriate bride for him. Listening to Sanjay's concerns, I asked him if he disapproved of arranged marriages. To my surprise, he said he didn't. He said the divorce rates within his community were low and that his own parents' marriage had been arranged. They had been married thirty years and had a loving, supportive union. Sanjay could see many benefits of arranged marriages and felt he would expect it of his own children, if he had any. All this left me wondering why he saw the arranged marriage as evidence of his parents' interference in his life.

Suddenly Sanjay asked me what I thought of gay people. I replied that it rather depended on their personalities. I said I had once had a gay neighbour who attacked my dog with a brush for leaving a calling card on his lawn! On the other hand his partner found it hysterical that my dog preferred their lawn to mine. Sanjay laughed and said, 'OK, I think I know where you are coming from'. Confident that his coach was non-judgmental, he revealed that he had known he was gay ever since he had been a small boy. To a certain extent the culture of his background made it easier to hide. His parents valued education and had been thrilled by Sanjay's years of studious labour. 'Plenty of time for girls later', they would say. Unfortunately it was now time.

Sanjay was convinced that his parents would disown him if they knew. And he was right: they did. It was a difficult decision to tell them and the consequences were very painful. But Sanjay could not live a lie and deceive either his parents or his chosen bride. Although saddened by his parents' decision, Sanjay remains pragmatic. 'I love my parents and believe they still love me. They are doing what they believe is right and I can not condemn them for that, any more than I can condemn myself for doing what I believe is right.'

Living by your values will not always have the dramatic outcome of Sanjay's situation. I have coached many clients who have hit less stormy waters. But this is one area where it would be careless to lure you into a false sense of security. You have to be prepared for the consequences. Melanie's life was made unhappy by ignoring values. I'll leave the last words to Sanjay. 'One day I hope to fall in love and have a partner. There was a time when this was a dream – now it's a goal.'

If you want to examine your values further, use your journal to write out the sort of values you are prepared to put yourself on the line for.

▪ Mission Statements

Sanjay was clear that, as well as having his values, his overall mission in life was to live by his own code of conduct. Establishing your own mission statements can help you to embrace your values and see the importance of having an overall sense of purpose. The term 'mission statement' is perhaps more commonly used in business, as an official statement that lays out the aims and objectives of that business. It's a term that I like to use in coaching. Once you have your values in place it's a lot easier to make mission statements. When you hear about someone being on a 'mission' it suggests commitment and passion. And that's exactly what you need. Making personal mission statements helps you to see the bigger picture. If you are a *Star Trek* fan, you might recall their mission statement at the start of the show: 'To boldly go where no man has gone before'. That's not a bad one to have. You might even want 'to seek out new civilisations'.

Think about the sort of mission statements you would like to make. These can be on any scale, whether large or small. Have a look at the list below:

- Make the world a better place

- Preserve the environment

- Stay on a spiritual path

- Travel the world

- Bring about world peace

- Go down in history

- Be the best at my job

- Always be there for my family

- Make a lot of money

- Continue to learn

- Fight for a political cause

- Respect myself and other people

- Enjoy life

Look at the seven areas of your life chart. Make some mission statements for each one. Read them on a regular basis, to remind you of the overall purpose of each one.

When I cover mission statements with clients, this is often where they choose to review their spiritual/religious forms. Perhaps the word 'mission' has some significance here. You may find basic questions about the meaning of life coming into your head, such as: What is the purpose of my life? Why am I here? Where am I going? Regardless of your particular convictions in this area, whether they are strong or – you believe – absent, give some thought to this area. Your coaching programme involves a great deal of self-exploration. It may change the way in which you define yourself and provoke further questions as to your role and purpose in life.

For some individuals their mission statement becomes the single and most significant aspect in their life. Mother Theresa dedicated her life to God and caring for the poor. Many rel-gious leaders have spent a lifetime in prayer and meditation, their mission being enlightenment. There is one thing for sure: having a mission in life gives you a sense of purpose.

▪ How To Establish Your Goals

Now that you understand your values and have made some mission statements, let's see how this relates to establishing your goals. If you have set goals, do they still seem relevant? Would you like to make any changes or add any new goals to your list? If you are still finding it a bit of a struggle, here is an additional exercise to help you on the way.

EXERCISE

1. Using every area of your life chart, list some goals that you think are worth achieving. They don't have to be goals that are relevant to you: it may help to have someone else in mind – a role model or person you admire.

Make the goals ambitious. There is no need to concern yourself about how they will be achieved. Be creative – let your imagination run wild. Let's have some fun here. I'll throw in a few for good measure.

- **Work/career** take over your nearest rival; open a chain of fashion boutiques

- **Health** join a gym; enter in next year's marathon

- **Friends/social life** increase my circle of friends; throw lavish dinner parties

- **Family** spend more time with my family; set clear boundaries with my family

- **Personal Relationships** get married; have children

- **Finances** start a pension plan; save 10 per cent of my salary

- **Spiritual and religious life** go to church/synagogue/mosque; meditate regularly

Got the hang of it? – Now off you go.

2. Now imagine how it would feel to be the person achieving a particular goal. Wouldn't you wake up every morning feeling motivated, enthusiastic, excited and raring to go?

Hold on to this feeling and it will help you to avoid the common mistake of talking yourself out of your goals. This often occurs before you even get the goal on paper. If you are in the habit of doing this, your goal becomes no more than a fleeting thought: an ideal daydream that is quickly discarded. What you need to do is make the goal real. It's really not difficult. Treat your goal as a seed. In order to nourish it, feed it with passionate thoughts. Acknowledge the goal with positive thoughts. Listing reasons why you can't achieve a goal will kill the seed. Remember: it's the new you that will be achieving the goal, so don't be concerned with the past.

3. Look at the list of goals you have identified in this exercise. Perhaps you have found a few more goals you could add to your forms. Keep the standards high. Unless a goal really pushes you to the limit, there's little fulfilment to be gained from achieving it.

The next chapter shows you how to stay in the right frame of mind to achieve your goals.

▪ Conclusion

► Define your values.

► Prioritise your values.

► Make some mission statements.

► Set goals that will push you to the limit.

CHAPTER THREE

Developing a Positive Mental Attitude

A RE YOU A POSITIVE person? Like me, you might have read books or articles on how to re-programme your mind, take control, think positive and so on. They sound great at first, don't they? But it's easy to stay positive when things are going well; not so easy when life seems to be sliding out of your control. You know those times in your life when well-meaning friends say: 'Look on the bright side!'. I used to think: It's easy for you to say that, you don't have my problems.

Then something struck me. I had always assumed that because I hadn't verbalised my response to my friends, there was obviously no damage done. But what about the damage I was doing to myself? At difficult times in my life, when I really needed to stay positive, I was my own worst enemy. Not only that, I was blocking out supportive remarks from friends. This chapter is about how to avoid all that.

▪ How Do You See Yourself?

EXERCISE

Start by getting out your journal. List three or four positive words you think would be used to describe you by:

1. A friend, who might describe you as loyal and trustworthy

2. A work colleague, who might describe you as co-operative and efficient

3. Your partner, who might describe you as loving and generous

4. A family member, who might describe you as reliable and responsible

Here's a tip: only select people you feel like or love you. If you feel really pushed, leave out a category.

Now list three or four words to describe how you see yourself as a friend, work colleague, partner and family member. Your descriptions are probably based on feedback you receive or an image of how you would like to be perceived. The real purpose of this exercise is to examine how you perceive yourself. Have you made equally positive remarks about yourself, or are some of them less positive than the other people's descriptions?

To sustain a positive mental attitude, your self-esteem needs to be high. If your self-esteem is low or tends to fluctuate, don't worry: this chapter will help you to improve it and keep it consistent. Basing self-esteem on the opinions of other people alone is not enough. Once you accept responsibility for your own self-esteem it becomes a whole lot easier to monitor and maintain. You are the one consistent force in your own life, so who better to rely on?

▪ Improving Your Self-Esteem

When your self-esteem is low the level of insecurity increases. Recalling school days, I'm sure you can think of a particular teacher whose approach was conducive to your development. Good teachers encourage and support pupils. They are aware of how fragile your confidence may be. An overly harsh remark can severely halt your progress. Confidence goes hand in hand with self-esteem. You will encounter many people who demonstrate little regard for your feelings. Harsh remarks will be made and the support you receive may even be limited at times. But it's up to you to fill in the blanks. As you remain the constant in your own life, stay consistent.

To increase your self-esteem, make a list of your achievements. Include every thing you can think of from swimming certificates to being first in the egg and spoon race at school. List future development skills. Rather than focus on what you haven't achieved, concern yourself with gaining the skills required for your future progress.

By now, you may have identified the changes you want to make. The nagging question 'Am I doing the right thing?' can hold you back. Seeking approval is understandable. But first you need to have self-approval. To do this, confirm your goals and values on a daily basis. To start with, this can be just reading them and visualising achieving them. This makes the goal feel real. Here are some techniques you can use to increase your visual image.

1. **Gather brochures and information** Let's say you have a goal to buy a new car, or go on holiday. Adding a brochure to your file brings the goal a bit closer. There might be a magazine article that you find inspiring. If so, cut it out and stick it in the file. The purpose of your file is to create a scene set in the future. The more magnificent it is, the greater your desire to get there. I was once called on to judge the beauty salon of the year award. Each salon entering had to produce a presentation folder. Some of those folders were just stunning. The salons look so inviting, not only did you want to go there, they left you with a sense of what it would actually be like. Treatment lists tempted you with soothing massages, pampering pedicures and uplifting facials.

   The same could be said of your life. If there's nothing of interest, why bother looking at it? For easy reference, divide your file into seven separate sections for each of the seven steps. As you start to work on your goals, continue adding to the file. Include things like acceptance letters, invitations, job applications, theatre tickets. Anything, in other words, that confirms your progress in each area.

2. **Visualisation** If you want your goal to become a reality, the first step is to make it real in your own mind. You can use visualisation to do this, but it must be positive visualisation. Since you have total freedom to predict the outcome, make sure it's a good one. The fear of disappointment may make you a bit cautious about letting your imagination run riot, but there's no room for pessimism in this exercise. Life does not always go according to

plan. But positive people remain optimistic and are better equipped to bounce back again. Have some fun in your own mind. Visualise people co-operating, opportunities presenting themselves, achieving your goals and how it would feel.

3. **Stay motivated** You can use thoughts to make a deposit in your motivational bank account, or a withdrawal. Keep your account in credit by filling it with positive thoughts. Have you ever come up with a really good idea and felt that little flutter of excitement, only to find a few days later it no longer seems such a good idea? Along the way you may have talked yourself out of it or allowed someone else to. You may have good reason to throw out a particular idea, but if you do it too much, your motivation will be sadly lacking.

4. **Enthusiasm is infectious** To make other people excited about your ideas or goals they need to see that *you* are. Ideas are like seeds, they require nurturing in order to withstand the elements. Feed them with positive affirmations, thoughts and visualisation, and watch the enthusiasm and motivation grow.

When I worked in the beauty industry, many of my clients were high-profile, household names, whether actors or models. You would think they'd be supremely confident, wouldn't you? Don't believe a word of it. Here were the people who were being praised to the skies by every magazine, photographer and TV show in town, and yet underneath all that surface beauty, they were bundles of nerves and insecurities.

For some observers, all this self-obsession and vanity was just too irritating for words. How could these beautiful people ignore the blessings nature had bestowed on them and harp on about some minute blemish or imaginary large bottom? But was that really fair? Doesn't it just tell us that, regardless of circumstances, abilities and appearance, self-esteem comes from within?

▪ Ask The Right Questions

When you are faced with a new challenge, it's tempting to look for reassurance from others. But, really, self-confirmation should come first, because the first questions we ask are to ourselves. When your self-esteem is high, you are far more likely to ask positive questions about yourself, such as, 'How can I improve my performance at work?' This is as opposed to a negative question such as, 'Why is my performance at work so poor?' Questions involving the word 'How' concentrate your mind on improving your performance, whereas the 'Why' questions keep you blocked with the problem. To see this at work, try asking yourself the question, 'How can I improve my self-esteem?' compared to, 'Why is my self-esteem so low?' The 'How' question will push you to look for ways to improve your self-esteem, whereas the 'Why' question is more likely to confirm your lack of self-esteem and throw in a few negative reasons in the process. The overall focus is in improving it, not trying to work out why it's low.

Positive thinking is not about anaesthetising emotions. If anything, it can put you in touch with your emotions and allow you to use them as a safety net.

You will already know how to ask the right questions if you have ever comforted a friend through a difficult situation.

A client called Sally told me that when she was trying to come to terms with the fact that her husband had left her, a so-called friend asked her: 'Do you think he left you because you were overweight?' Sally had been persecuting herself with the question about her weight. The level of pain she experienced eventually became so great that she had to find a way to deal with it. And she did. On a daily basis she would write out a list of all her positive qualities, each day adding a few more to the list. Once the list was complete, she would read it aloud over and over again. To begin with it felt contrived, but Sally persevered and gradually began to feel more positive about herself.

How do you think you could have prepared Sally to deal with the initial tactless remark? Assume that this is a person you care about: a friend or loved one. They are reeling from the snub, and your job is to coach them through this crisis. Spend a few minutes thinking about what you would say before reading on.

It's only natural to want to defend someone you care about. Attack is a common form of defence and you may feel inclined to attack the person who made the remark. That may temporarily distract the person in pain, but will it be effective in the long run? Another approach is to offer words of comfort and reassurance. You could point out all their worthy qualities, the ones that make them such a special person. Can you imagine how frustrating it would be if your words fell on deaf ears and only the unpleasant remark registered? If Sally hadn't learnt to adopt a positive approach to the problem by affirming her self-esteem, she might have endured years of pain from that one callous remark. The same thing can happen to you when you hold on to the negative.

Thinking negatively is a bad habit, but you can break it. First, you need to recognise it. Stating that you want to be positive is a step in the right direction, but to achieve it you need to monitor your thoughts. Think about the words of reassurance you offered to Sally. The aim was not to aggravate her discomfort. It makes sense to have an awareness of the unnecessary pain that can be self-inflicted.

▪ Putting the Theory into Practice

Try these techniques every day: you'll soon notice the difference.

1. **Police your thoughts** To do this you have to remain constantly vigilant about what and how you think. Be equally careful about the thoughts you have that relate to other people. For example a colleague at work makes a silly mistake and you find yourself thinking: 'What an idiot'. Next time, when *you* make the mistake and you think you're the idiot, you'll know then why a better alternative is: 'We all make mistakes – who doesn't?' If you are inclined to think and speak negatively about others, the chances are you will become your own victim before long.

2. **Convert the negative to the positive** Every time you find yourself thinking negatively – STOP. Be aware and make a conscious decision to change that thought to a positive one. To begin with you may find that no more than five minutes elapse before you have to stop. As you progress, thinking positively becomes a habit.

3. **Handling problems** If problems are blocking your progress, write them down: they look less threatening on paper. It helps to let out some of the emotional steam associated with them. Once they are on paper, look at them as if you had a puzzle in front of you. I may say this a few times in the course of the book, but a puzzle requires a solution or formula, whereas a problem calls for an answer. You won't get answers by asking the same questions or using the same approach.

4. **Ask the right questions** The brain will always try and find an answer, regardless of the questions you ask. It's better to ask the right questions, which means asking positive ones. So imagine you are trying to solve the puzzle. Ask yourself: 'Why can't I solve this puzzle?' Are you getting any positive or useful answers back? Now try asking yourself: 'How can I solve this problem?' Do you see the difference? Now you're asking the brain for some contribution to move forward with. This analogy can be applied to problems, too. Asking 'Why is this happening to me?' is counter-productive, whereas 'How can I turn this situation around, how can I make it work for me?' pushes you into solution mode. We will do some more work on this in the next chapter.

5. **Watch your terminology** When my clients work on positive mental thinking, I monitor what they say very carefully. Sometimes, as an exercise, they agree to let me interrupt them if they are making negative statements. They might only get out a few sentences before I say: 'STOP'. Although they have agreed to let me do it, it startles them. After a few minutes of having me hollering 'STOP', they begin to think more carefully before speaking. Initially this slows them down, but the pace quickly resumes. Clients often remark how unaware they had been about the negative communication they used. Not only that, but when they change their terminology it also changes their mood.

I'll give you a few examples of how conversations change. 'I can't think of any goals' – STOP. 'I'm working on setting goals … I'm fed up being so undermined at work' – STOP. 'My work situation could be better, I need to finds ways to improve it … It doesn't matter what I do, my partner never listens to me' –

STOP. 'I need to find more effective ways to communicate with my partner.' And so on.

There are times when it is not immediately obvious to clients why I have stopped them. For example, with the statement 'I can't think of any goals', one client said, 'I'm not being negative, I'm just stating a fact'. Would you want to be stuck with that fact if you were trying to set goals? Setting goals is not always easy, so why make it harder by telling yourself you can't do it? Study the first statements carefully and you will see why they can keep you blocked. Constantly stating discontent will not improve your situation or state of mind.

Practise communicating your problems without presenting a hopeless case. Positive thinkers speak positively. So be selective in your choice of words.

6. **Use affirmations** Affirmations are wonderful for boosting self-esteem and confidence because although initially you may not believe them and they feel contrived, your subconscious mind will accept them and feed them back into your conscious mind. If you are in the habit of talking or thinking yourself into a corner, start setting some positive affirmations which are specific to your situation, e.g. 'I am committed to setting goals and achieving them; I am committed to coaching myself'. Use every opportunity to affirm yourself by constantly being supportive. The minute you think 'I can't do this', replace it with 'I can do it and I will'. There are some very good books on affirmation that will get you in the right frame of mind (see Further Reading).

Let's explore some of these techniques in more detail and look at other applications you may find useful.

▪ Change Your Past – Change Your Future

Coaching is normally concerned with moving forward and there is not a great deal of emphasis on past events and experiences. But how easy would you find it to ignore your own past? If you enrolled on a coaching programme and were told not to mention your past, I think you would feel pretty short-changed. The past has relevance to your future and I firmly believe that coaching techniques have a role in both.

Because you are the historian to your own past, you have the power to change a negative memory into a positive memory. I'm not asking you to rewrite history and falsify memories, just to revisit it using the right coaching questions. For example, if your recollection of your schooldays is full of unhappy memories, no matter how bleak they actually were, when you ask the question, 'What do I recall that was good about them?' you will search for a positive event. And as you continue with that line of thought, you may come up with several such events. What was once just a bad memory will be balanced with some good memories. To give a fair and accurate account of past events you can review them with a new focus – a positive one.

You can try a little experiment here in re-writing history. To help you do that I'd like to tell you about Marsha.

Marsha was keen to be coached. Initially, her reasons for coaching seemed to be to talk about past traumas, and I was concerned that coaching might not provide her with the space to review that part of her life. Other forms of counselling and therapy encourage this approach, and it is always appropriate to give a client a choice that allows an informed decision. You will only make changes when you are ready. My concern with Marsha was that she was not ready to move forward.

Marsha was prone to talking about her past. She had had a difficult childhood. Her father was a dogmatic character and her mother was the eternal martyr, always reminding Marsha of the sacrifices she made and how Marsha's father ruined everyone's life, especially her mother's. This did not appear a subject matter to be tackled in coaching, with statements like leave your past behind and let's focus on your future. Marsha wanted to adopt a positive mental attitude, but the past kept getting in the way. She was desperate to move forward and refused to use other avenues available. I am eternally grateful to the contribution Marsha made to my work by her perseverance to be coached. This is what happened.

We began by working through the principles of positive mental thinking. Marsha was encouraged to ask herself new questions that related to her current situation. So rather than ask things like 'Why is my life this way? Why do I have these problems?', the questions changed to 'How can I make this work for me? How can I move forward?' Marsha made progress and could see how the right questions moved her forward. However, during our conversations, she was still inclined to go off on a tangent and talk about the past. On one such occasion she said: 'What a shame my father never tried this.'

I was interested by that so I said: 'Tell me something positive about your father'. Marsha was momentarily startled by my response. 'Well, he was a very good cook,' she said, haltingly. With a bit more prompting, Marsha relayed the following: 'My dad was the best cook; mum was a bit of a disaster in that area. I don't think she enjoyed cooking, so dad did most of it. He used to take so much trouble remembering what we all liked and didn't like. He could grill a piece of toast that melted in your mouth. I remember sitting on the sofa at night with a mug of tea and slice of toast. Dad washed my school socks and would hang them in front of the fire'. As I fired more questions at her, Marsha continued to relay childhood memories. It was not so much a case of history being rewritten as revisited. Questions play a major role in your mental well-being. You use them to get information about yourself, life, experiences, the past and the future. Our sessions continued, with Marsha feeling much happier about herself, her past, and her future.

At the initial coaching session, I like to provide clients with space to talk. They are asked questions about themselves; my role is that of the prompting listener. You may be wondering what this has to do with a chapter on positive mental thinking? Well, the majority of clients describe themselves as being positive. Yet when discussing problems few demonstrate an ability to remain positive.

Living the life you truly desire does not involve a problem-free existence. I remember working in a geriatric hospital when I was eighteen years old. The ward was a long-stay unit for patients considered beyond rehabilitation and physiotherapy. Walking on to that ward every morning, I felt that I had my whole life before me. Yet elderly people awaiting their departure from life surrounded me. The atmosphere was not as gloomy as you may think. Imagine walking into such a situation and being greeted with: 'Hello Eileen, lovely morning isn't it?' I was deeply moved by the ability of some of the patients to remain cheerful. How could this be? Lifetimes of experiences were often mapped out on their faces and yet one thing set a few apart – their positive attitude. There was no evidence of a charmed life prior to hospitalisation and little to distinguish their prevailing circumstances.

There are situations in life that may be beyond your control, but the mind has a benevolent predisposition that both invites and allows control. Taking control is not an easy discipline for you to learn – the good ones rarely are. Taking responsibility for your life is open to various interpretations. Perhaps the essential ingredient to your state of mind is achieved by asking yourself the right questions.

▪ Police Your Subconscious Mind

Your brain attempts to find an answer to every question posed. A negative question often leads to a negative answer. Such is the power of the subconscious mind that if you firmly plant a message it can become more real than any subsequent intellectual reasoning.

The subconscious mind does not distinguish between what is real and not real. Your conscious mind presents information that the subconscious assumes is real. Here is an example of just how powerful it is.

Gerry bought a converted barn in the country to use as a weekend retreat.

The only problem was that during the week the barn kept getting broken into. Because of the remote location of the barn, even the alarm system did not deter the intruders. So Gerry came up with what he thought was a great idea. He painted several large signs and positioned them around the outside of the premises. They read: 'WARNING – THIS PROPERTY CONTAINS LIVE SNAKES. IN THE EVENT THAT YOU ARE BITTEN, PLEASE CONTACT THE LONDON HOSPITAL FOR TROPICAL DISEASES.'

I don't know the legalities of this, but the deterrent worked.

From the minute the signs were put up his barn was safe from intruders. Gerry congratulated himself on his resourceful plan and prepared for a relaxing weekend in his secluded sanctuary.

That weekend, something disturbed him. There seemed to be an unusual activity in the grass outside: strange rustlings and shapes mysteriously appeared. A discarded piece of hose-pipe made him jump out of his skin. By Sunday morning Gerry decided to return to London. He was feeling tense and put it down to some unfinished paperwork.

The following weekend he returned to the barn. This time he didn't even make it to the front door. Despite the fact that all sense of logic told him otherwise, he could not contend with the thought that there might be snakes lurking in the shadows.

So strong was the resulting phobia that Gerry eventually sold his barn.

Developing a phobia like this is obviously an extreme reaction. Nevertheless it does suggest that you need to monitor your thought processes and be careful about the information you could inadvertently feed in. You may know on one level that you are perfectly capable of doing something and yet somewhere along the line you have questioned your ability. Perhaps it's so bad that you draw a mental blank over the simplest tasks. Clients of mine, including the managing directors of multinational companies who are very competent at their jobs, have told me how incompetent they become in certain situations. It can be due to pressure, the attitude of a particular colleague, a joke or careless remark that somehow hits their insecurity button.

▪ Coaching Buddies

You're on a mission – a mission to change your life. The first half of this book deals with survival techniques. The aim is to reach your destination and achieve your goals fully intact. Before embarking on any journey it's always a good idea to be prepared for any eventuality, which means stocking up on provisions. If you fancied a trekking trip and had never previously been on one, you could accompany someone who had. At the very least, you would want to talk to them and gain the benefit of their experience. There are lots of people to help you on your journey, so let's do some work enlisting coaching buddies.

What makes a coaching buddy? Well, we probably assume that they're people who give constant support, understanding and empathy. Some of your coaching buddies will be like that. But, surprisingly, not all of them are. A coaching buddy is a catalyst, and you might find that the most unlikely characters are going to be involved in your future progress, even if they are people you don't think of as friends.

For whatever reason, you have been prompted to make changes in your life. Some of the people in your life have a vested interest in keeping you where you are. This is not as sinister as it sounds. They may well like you the way you are and feel less able to embrace the new you. However, you want to change. And change you will. Life is not stationary, and experiences do make an impact. Doing what's right for you will not necessarily meet with everyone's approval.

I say this because it would be all too easy to surround yourself with 'Yes' people. Sometimes hearing what you don't want to hear makes the difference. Loved ones can deliver a few home truths for all the right reasons. Enemies deliver them for all the wrong reasons. That's not to say they are less effective. Someone who sets out to do you a disservice could unintentionally do you a service. Even if it's the time you get really mad and say 'Enough is enough', it might be the kick-start you need to take action. Bestowing on them the title 'coaching buddy' gives you the power to remain positive about the situation. The underlying message here is balance, which has to be maintained in all extremes. To put your positive mental attitude to the test you have to experience both extremes and still remain positive.

The approach I take differs from that of many other professionals and practising coaches. They often encourage clients to eliminate those around them who are not supportive, be they friends or family. When I went into business, my sister relayed a conversation she had had with my mother. Its theme was 'When is Eileen going to get a proper job?'. As you will gather they were not a hundred per cent supportive. Although I believed their concerns were truly genuine, I still missed their support.

How would you have reacted? Would it have made you more determined to prove them wrong, or would you have fallen at the first hurdle? Well, my own desire was to prove myself right. There was no emphasis on proving others wrong. There are those in your life who truly love you and care about you. Just because they withhold support does not mean they withhold love. They can make the wrong decision for all the right reasons, just as there are those who make the right decision for all the wrong reasons. The important factor has to be your interpretation of the situation. You don't have to go it alone, but be prepared for a degree of self-sufficiency. Only then will you truly recognise your coaching buddies.

▪ Conclusion

▶ Define yourself positively. Write out a few positive statements and use them on a daily basis to affirm your commitment to your goals.

▶ Ask the right questions.

▶ Police your thoughts. Take care of the information you feed into your subconscious mind.

▶ Be aware of negative cycles and when you are putting yourself down.

▶ Watch your terminology – not just what you say about yourself, but what you say about other people.

▶ To build self-esteem, list your achievements. List future development skills.

▶ Use your folder to create an exciting future.

▶ Use positive visualisation.

▶ Stay motivated.

▶ Look out for coaching buddies.

CHAPTER FOUR

Creating a Mental Oasis and Problem Solving Zone

OW GOOD ARE YOU at dealing with problems? May be it depends what sort of a problem you're having to deal with. I'm not referring to monumental travesties, or political decisions that affect humanity on a grand scale. I'm talking about the sort of problems we encounter on a day-to-day basis.

What seems like the most enormous hurdle to one person may be a mere blip to someone else, so there's little point judging one problem against another. In coaching, I never try to weigh up what constitutes a problem. I prefer to concentrate on the level of concern or anxieties experienced and then set about seeing how to minimise it. Whatever causes you concern demands your attention.

One of the great benefits about being coached is that it gives you someone to act as a sounding board to your problems. The coach can remain impartial and be pragmatic about other people's problems, because they are not affected by them. What if you were able to take the same approach to your own problems: can you imagine how much easier it would be to find solutions?

The essence of this chapter is to find a way of working through your problems without draining your internal resources so that you can achieve your goals. Problems are a useful and necessary part of your development. They can reveal things that you may not otherwise see, which is why I teach that you must treat them as an essential and inevitable interruption in your life. Don't waste time asking: 'Why me?' It's more useful to ask how you can deal with them.

▪ The Emotional Link

There is a certain comfort in knowing what comes next. Few individuals go through life always expecting the unexpected. A friend of mine who is a highly sought-after psychic adviser told me that new clients are often quick to tell her, 'I don't actually believe in this stuff', although the one thing that brings them to her is a problem. For whatever reason, they suddenly want to know what comes next. They seek reassurance that everything is going to be all right.

Problems make us feel out of control. Removing the comfort zone of predictability makes you feel like you're in free-fall, with nothing to guarantee a smooth landing. When the discomfort factor becomes too great, you start questioning your previous belief patterns and searching for new options.

The techniques we are going to work on in this chapter are as follows:

► changing your running order;

► taking responsibility for a problem;

► dealing with the cause not the symptom;

► being a player and a spectator;

► creating a mental oasis and problem-solving zone.

My information is not presented as being conclusive. I say that because whilst I truly believe in the effectiveness of the techniques you are about to work on, I also think there is a unique message for you in every problem you encounter.

These techniques are your building blocks. You experience problems on a very personal level so you have to give yourself permission to think about your problem, and experience the emotions related to it. Staying positive is not a process of denying how you truly feel. By trusting your instincts your emotions can become a safety net. They can work for you. With my clients it has become apparent that at one end of the scale, problems cause some people to be locked into painful emotions long after the event, whilst at the other end there is a process of denial that causes some individuals to run from their emotions and at times from life itself. To avoid either extreme there has to be a conscious decision to shift gear mentally. Take a new approach: that's the focus of my work.

Problems can and often do cause pain, and there is a natural temptation to look for the magic, problem-free formula. Well, I don't personally prescribe to a problem-free existence. All my clients are encouraged to face their predicaments head on, but I also stress that coaching is not a dependency relationship. You are very much in the driving seat. Rather than hit the same old wall every time, the aim is to re-route you when necessary and get you back on track as quickly as possible.

▪ Changing the Running Order

I'm sure you're familiar with this phenomenon: half-way through reading a newspaper article or hearing a friend tell a story your brain is racing ahead to predict what comes next, or what it thinks should come next. That sequence of events is based on how you see the world. Problems stop that sequence and interfere with your running order. In order to get back on track you need a solution. This may explain why what presents itself as a problem to one person is not a problem to another – their running order is different and they perceive no interference.

So if you have a very restricted running order, it makes sense that you will encounter more interference and problems. There is one very common denominator that precedes a restricted running order, and that is a reluctance or fear of change.

Surely, you may say, the more changes I make in my life, the more problems I am likely to encounter? Well, not necessarily. If you decide to make changes, that creates a new running order. The more changes you make, the more potential running orders you have. You will still experience problems, but can you see the level of flexibility you have? Let's say you have recently approached a magazine with an idea for a short story, and to your surprise the editor of the magazine likes your story. The only trouble is, she doesn't like the ending and wants you to write a new one. Obviously you know the characters involved in the story, so it's important to create an ending that's reflective of them and doesn't compromise your work. You can use as many possible endings as you like, according to how you want the running order to be. You can do the same in your own life too.

Similarly, if you had a goal to get fit, and decided to take up jogging, but in the course of achieving your goal you suffer an ankle strain, by changing your running order, e.g. by taking up swimming, you can realise your goal to get fit.

The minute you make a conscious effort to practise positive thinking, the running order changes. Rather than hitting that wall again and experiencing the same old negative emotions that blocked your progress, you are looking for a contingency plan. In other words, your brain shifts to solution mode.

Summary

▶ It's better to keep the goal at the forefront of your mind and view problems as a necessary challenge to overcome along the way.

▶ Problems are an inevitable part of daily life.

▶ There is no definitive rule that states that your goals will be achieved without resistance.

▶ Accepting the inevitability of problems puts you in the best frame of mind to find solutions.

▪ Taking Responsibility for a Problem

The way in which you define a problem will obviously affect how you deal with it. If you look at your coaching forms (at the back of the book) there is a category for Immediate challenges/blocks/ problems. The word block is very significant because your whole being, physical and mental, is at a standstill when you are blocked. The way to get round it is to think 'Why am I having this problem?'

You may not be under any illusions about having been promised a charmed life, but some people still find it hard to accept that life doesn't always go according to plan. Just as you have your own particular agenda, so does everyone else. Just as you are prone to changing your mind, so are others. What was once a shared goal may no longer remain one. If everyone had the same running order we'd all have the same problems, or lack of them. Obviously that's not the case, so problems remain something to be dealt with on a daily basis.

You'd think that, when you experience problems so frequently, you'd be less likely to be stuck with the same old problems. Accepting that problems go with the territory stops you asking the 'Why me?' questions. Life is not out to get you; it's just a case of recognising that mutual synchronicity causes few interruptions to your running order, while a lack of it does. The real solution is to take responsibility for your problems and not resort to blaming other people.

▪ Deal With the Cause – Not the Symptom

When identifying problems it's easy to get caught up in what would best be described as the symptoms. So in the Family/ extended family section the statement 'My mother keeps interfering with my life' appears. Constant interference would indeed cause a problem. But the underlying issue stems from a breakdown in a relationship and the overstepping of boundaries. If you hand over the focus of a problem to another person, even if they are the cause of it, you might end up by expecting them to deal with it. But what if they perceive their interference as being helpful or making a useful contribution to your life? Put that way, there's not much chance of them dealing with that, is there? What about the protests you keep making? Well, if they haven't worked in the past, don't expect them to in the future. The body can become immune to a particular type of medicine and likewise the same old solutions to dealing with a problem become ineffective. A change of strategy is required.

Siobhan came to me for coaching because she was sick and tired of her mother-in-law's interference. Although Siobhan was convinced she had tried several different approaches in dealing with the problem, she had always viewed the problem as being with her mother-in-law. In the past, Siobhan had reacted to the symptoms of the problem, which were mainly her immense frustration at what she described as her mother-in-law's total lack of respect and inability to respond to Siobhan's protests. Redefining the problem allowed Siobhan to take responsibility for dealing with it, and find a workable solution, so whereas she had initially stated the problem as being: 'My mother-in-law keeps interfering in my life', she changed this to 'I have a problem setting clear boundaries with my mother-in-law and dealing with her behaviour.' This is a subtle change, but by bringing the problem back to herself, Siobhan's focus moved to dealing with the cause of the problem – i.e. boundaries – and to intervening before the problem developed.

Siobhan's mother-in-law had a habit of telephoning ten minutes before yet another uninvited visit. Previously, Siobhan would spend the afternoon fuming about the unwelcome interruption to her day. With her new boundaries in place, she was able to make it clear to her mother-in-law that it was inconvenient. Initially, her mother-in-law sulked and was inclined to respond with comments like; 'Oh well if you don't want to see me ...' To which Siobhan kept up a friendly yet consistent response on the lines of 'We love seeing you but it's not convenient today'. After a few weeks, her mother-in-law got the message and recognised Siobhan's new boundaries.

What you need to do, as Siobhan did, is settle the issue of ownership. Bring the situation back to yourself and take possession of the problem. What I mean by that is be clear about how it affects you and the part you play in the situation. If you think you play no part, then you are excluding yourself from finding a solution. When Siobhan brought this problem back to herself, the difference this remark made was to put herself back in the driving seat. There are bound to be times when people interfere in your life. The options are: put up with it, moan about it, play the victim and be at the mercy of others. Or deal with it by finding a solution to the problem.

Getting caught up in why people behave the way they do provides no quick answers. If you wanted to get to the bottom of why your mother interferes in your life, you'll find yourself reduced to speculation and hypothesis. Even if you think you have found the answer, it won't remove the problem. By keeping your focus on the issue of boundaries, you prompt yourself to seek a solution.

▪ Being a Player and a Spectator

EXERCISE

The Spectator

I am going to suggest an exercise in which you are that spectator, that impartial bystander. If you work through it, you will soon see how looking at other people's problems can help you with your own problems, if you take the techniques you are about to develop and then apply them to your own problems.

Here are some problems that people often voice:

1. My partner is not supportive.

2. My boss treats me badly.

3. Friends take advantage of me.

All these are problems in their own way, I'm sure you'll agree, but look at the language: the emphasis is always on the other person. To exert any real control and find a workable solution the emphasis has to be on you. So let's look as these problems in more detail. Use your journal to list some possible solutions for each of the above problems. Write down as many things as you can, without spending too long on it.

How are you shaping up with solutions? Having tried this technique with clients, I'll give you a few of their answers:

▪ **Problem 1** Find a new partner. Ask for support. Learn to be less dependent on your partner. Tell your partner how you feel. Seek the support you need from others.

▪ **Problem 2** Talk to your boss about how you feel. Get a new job. Stand up for yourself. Ignore the boss. Improve your performance at work. Report the boss to a superior. Tell the boss their behaviour is unacceptable.

- **Problem 3** Get some new friends. Set clear boundaries. Tell your friends you don't like their behaviour. Stop trying to please them.

As you can see the solutions offered are varied. Whether or not any of them is the right solution depends on whether they remove the problem. A solution is right when it is right for you. You are seeking the best possible outcome to your own problems, so why not make that your starting point? Now it's time to change to being the active player.

The Player

Review the problems again. This time put yourself in the role of the player, which means imagining the problem affects you. Now the solutions on offer appear differently. You may not want a new job, or to tackle a boss head on. But if you are encountering this problem on a daily basis you must find a solution. Keep thinking about the best possible outcome and write it down. Visualise it happening. Make this image strong in your mind. Without worrying at this stage how you will achieve it, ask yourself the question: 'Do I believe this outcome is achievable?'

If you believe it is, you will start to work on the 'How' bit, i.e. how to make it happen, and your brain will back you up. On the other hand, if you don't believe your chosen solution is possible, the problem will remain with you. Wanting to change a situation is not enough. If you don't believe in your own solutions they remain unrealistic and unachievable. The problem becomes something that affects you. You become entirely passive, so the message you give to yourself is: 'There's nothing I can do.' You are the suffering spectator to your own problems.

The answer is to get back in the game and become the player. If a solution doesn't work, try a new manoeuvre, or work on your strategy. Problems get the better of you when you constantly opt for the spectator position. The spectator is a useful position enabling you to stand back and look for a solution to your problem, but you have to become the player to put your solution into action.

Summary

- ▶ Identify the root cause of the problem rather than getting distracted by the symptoms.

- ▶ When identifying a problem – bring it back to yourself and recognise it's up to you to find a solution.

- ▶ Think about your running order. Is it flexible? Does it need to change in order to achieve your goals? How is it affected by problems?

- ▶ For a solution to be realistic, you have to believe it is.

- ▶ View your problem as the spectator and list possible solutions.

- ▶ If a solution is right for you, become the active player and put it into effect.

You now have a working format that allows you to deal with problems. You can use this to successfully impose and closely monitor your own deadlines for problem solving. They involve you allocating a time to think about a problem, find a solution and put the plan into action. It is surprising how little time is specifically allocated to dealing with problems. They get jumbled up with other thoughts that also need space and refuse to go away. Instead, they pop up in your mind when you least expect them, and when they're least welcome.

Then there is 'talk time', the time you spend talking about a problem. It can be a great outlet allowing you to get something off your chest and mentally unload. It can gain you much needed support or help to put a new perspective on the situation and lead to a solution. Some problems are just begging for a solution and the more you talk about them the more they invite one, but of course talking won't always solve the problem.

So let's get to work on creating some space for solutions.

▪ Creating a Mental Oasis

EXERCISE

You could use your journal for this exercise. Spend a few minutes recalling an event that gives you the feel-good factor. It could be a good film, your favourite meal, intimate time with a loved one, a beautiful day. You are looking for a memory that puts you in a relaxed frame of mind and one that is easy to conjure up in your head. Once you have chosen an event, write it down in your journal. To make the imagery stronger, create as detailed a picture as possible. It helps to bring the senses into play, so recall smell, taste, sound, colours and sensations.

You will use this memory as your mental oasis: a place to enter, leave and re-enter.

It's worth setting some time aside – say ten minutes a day for the next few days – to focus on your mental oasis, to get in the habit of quickly tuning into it. Some of my clients find it helps to prepare their surroundings, i.e. find a quiet area where you won't be interrupted, play some relaxing music, remove any tight-fitting clothing, sit in a comfortable chair, spend a few minutes concentrating on your breathing. Once you can easily conjure up your mental oasis, move on to the next stage.

▪ Entering a Problem

EXERCISE

1. Using your journal, list the problems you would like to work on.

2. Spend a few minutes focusing on your mental oasis.

3. Now enter a current problem. Spend no more than five minutes thinking about the problem.

4. Write down your thoughts, feelings and emotions in your journal.

5. Watch your breathing. Breathing in through your nose and out through your mouth will calm the body and relax you.

6. Go back to your mental oasis for a few minutes.

7. Now go back to the problem, but this time focus on possible solutions. Think about the best possible outcome for you.

8. List your solutions.

9. Go back to your mental oasis for a few minutes.

10. Spend a few minutes thinking about your solutions again. This time, visualise achieving them.

11. Finally – spend a few minutes in your mental oasis.

To begin with, it may be easier to practise this technique first thing in the morning or towards the end of the day. These tend to be the times when problems flood your mind. So in order to get a good night's sleep or get the day off to a good start, use this technique. It requires discipline on your part. Allocate specific problems that you will only work on and think about in your mental oasis. As you become more proficient, use this technique at any convenient time during the day. To get the best from it, make sure you select a time when you can think clearly, without interruptions.

You may well find that during the switch from mental oasis to problem, the cross-over stage is when solutions are most likely to come to mind. But don't use this technique when you are about to go to sleep. If you drift off to sleep thinking about a problem, you may be in for a rough night.

Although this is a very simple technique, the results are dramatic. The brain quickly recognises the signals you are giving it. What you are doing is allowing yourself to set aside the much-needed time to deal specifically with a problem. As you continue to practise, thinking about problems at inopportune moments happens less often. They start to wait their turn. I can only tell you that it works.

When James came to me as a client, he identified no specific problem but saw coaching as a way of improving his all-round performance. However, when James filled in his forms he scored highly in every area except his Personal relationship form. Despite the fact that James had a girlfriend, he had scored a mere 3.

Interestingly, he had listed no goals or problems in this area, which made me curious.

James owned a very successful information technology company. Much of his day was spent in problem-solving mode and he wasn't keen on the idea of setting aside more time to deal with specific problems. After all, he could deal with them when they came up. During the course of James' coaching programme I requested that he use the mental oasis to set some goals in his personal relationship chart. Although I sensed some reluctance on his part, I knew that he wasn't the sort of person to walk away from a challenge as he prided himself on his ability to tackle any problem.

I'll let James take over the story from here, in his own words.

'I was surprised by all the forms but I rather enjoyed filling them in. It was no problem setting goals; I've done that all my life. I raced through every form until I got to Personal relationships. It would have been more fun filling in a tax return. To tell you the truth, I just couldn't be bothered. I hoped Eileen wouldn't notice, but she did.

'I highlighted the area with a low score but as soon as I had done it I kicked myself for not sticking a 10 down in the chart. Still, never being one to backtrack, I left it and moved on. Then used a mental oasis to set goals in my personal relationships. I really felt like I was being stretched.

'Off I went, five evenings a week, thinking happy thoughts before entering my problem – I couldn't set any goals in my personal relationships. The pressure mounted daily, I didn't fancy the prospect of going back to Eileen with no goals, so I stayed with it.

'I couldn't believe the things I was writing in my journal. The word 'lonely' kept reappearing, along with phrases like 'No one to talk to', 'no support' and 'no love'. Every time I focused on this one particular area, the same old stuff kept coming up. Finally, late one evening and with a bit of Dutch courage inside me, I wrote out some goals.

- The love of a strong woman

- Someone I can talk to and be vulnerable with

- To get married

- To have children

'Then I listed some problems:

- I don't want to be the eternal problem solver

- I'm sick to death of attracting women with problems

- I keep going out with vulnerable women because I'm afraid to appear vulnerable

'I looked at my list the next morning, my pen poised to scribble it out. But I couldn't; the words rang true. I had got through to my inner core, to the truth about me. At my next coaching session it was still there, and we were able to start dealing with it. You could say I got more than I bargained for. But I'll tell you something: it's not difficult being honest with your coach. The hardest part was being honest with myself. And now I am dealing with it.'

As you can see the mental oasis is very versatile.

▪ Conclusion

▶ Allocate time to deal with problems.

▶ Practise using your mental oasis on a daily basis.

▶ If problems spring to mind during the day, remind yourself that you have set aside time to deal with them.

▶ Always remember to write solutions down, otherwise you might forget them.

▶ Refer to a solution a few times. If it still looks like the best option, chances are it is.

CHAPTER FIVE

No More Excuses

YOU MAY HAVE HEARD of Roger Black: he certainly has a formidable track record. An Olympic and world 400 metre silver medallist, twice European and also Commonwealth champion as well as the world 400 metre relay gold medallist, he became the Great Britain athletics team captain and was awarded an MBE. A pretty impressive list of achievements, you will no doubt agree, but what makes Roger's achievements all the more exceptional is the fact that he suffers from a heart condition.

Throughout Roger's career as an international athlete, his condition remained a secret, only known to family, close friends and his doctors. 'I just didn't want to make it an issue,' he later said. 'And I didn't want to have an excuse if I failed.'

If he had revealed his physical frailty, nobody would have been that surprised if he had failed to shine on the field of sport, and yet, despite his problems, he still chose to compete in a discipline that requires maximum physical fitness. I've always had great admiration for sporting legends, but if one thing really makes Roger stand out in my mind it's his attitude. You see, I'm big on excuses. Not on making them, but on blowing them out of the water.

Excuses are the little voices in our heads telling us why we can't do something. To some people, they are 'the voice of reason', but I don't think much of that description. As an experiment, try substituting the word 'Excuse' every time you want to use the word 'Reason'. I think you'll find you don't get the same comfort factor from it. It certainly seems to unsettle clients when we're talking.

'Well, the reason I'm not doing so and so, Eileen, is because of such and such.' 'OK if you want to make that your excuse.' 'No – it's not an excuse it's a reason.'

I prefer to throw in the word excuse because it gets a reaction. It makes you question your decisions, be aware of the choices you have made and see that any given situation presents an option. It would be easy to think that the options are made for you, that fate has played a hand and the choices before you are limited. Coaching yourself means not taking that easy option.

The 'Why' question becomes useful the minute you start to ask 'Why not?' Presented with a challenge, you can either slip into a mind-set that looks for umpteen reasons as to why it is not achievable, or one that looks for ways to overcome the challenge. The distinguishing factor is attitude. Which one will you choose?

▪ Put Your Attitude to the Test

People who achieve goals stand out through attitude, through their determination to succeed even against the odds. That involves not only seizing opportunities but also creating them. Fall back on excuses and you could spend a lifetime regretting what might have been, and replacing your original excuse with 'if only'.

One obvious cause of excuses is fear. If you keep giving yourself reasons for not doing something, the chances are you won't do it. Getting rid of excuses should be easy, but just to get you in the mood, here are some warm-up exercises.

EXERCISE

Select one form from your life chart area that includes some goals. Divide a page in your journal in two halves and draw a vertical line down the middle. Write out a goal across the top of the page. On the right-hand side list as many reasons as you can for achieving that goal. On the left-hand side of the page list all the reasons you can think of for not achieving your goal.

It doesn't matter whether one list is longer than the other. What counts is what you make of the list. It may look something like this.

GOAL To get promotion at work

Reasons for not achieving	*Reasons for achieving*
Not that good at my job.	I'm determined to be good at my job and earn promotion
I don't have the necessary qualifications	I will gain the necessary qualifications
I'm not the best candidate.	I'm the most determined candidate

Do you see how all your apparent weaknesses can be converted into opportunities? You can't deal with weaknesses by ignoring them, crossing your fingers and hoping for the best. Now is the time to be up-front about them and find a way to turn them into strengths. If you are determined to succeed, you will, so long as you have your goals clearly in mind.

Goals take you into new territory. Do you remember your first day in a new job? Remember how unnerving, even hostile, that unfamiliar environment was? And yet, miraculously, by the end of the week it appeared so much less daunting. You adapt, you unwind a bit, you get to know people, to know your way around. Setting out on your goal can feel like that first day: opening the door on something new it's all too easy to feel tempted to run back to the security of familiar ground.

Tom was a client of mine whose goal was to get married. As far as he was concerned there was only one reason that stopped him asking his girlfriend. In his own words, she had 'a commitment problem.' After a little probing, it emerged that Tom had never actually got round to asking her to marry him, but as he was so keen to get married, we discussed his options.

Tom considered the possibility that the problem was of his own making. 'I think I fear rejection if my girlfriend says no,' he told me. 'I'll also be faced with the prospect of ending the relationship. I really want to get married and I don't know what's worse – knowing the answer, or not knowing.' Tom couldn't be sure of the outcome until he had popped the question, but as long as he remained adamant that the problem lay with his girlfriend, there was little chance of fulfilling his goal in this relationship. Tom was helped through his dilemma by focusing on his goal and reminding himself how important it was to him. He worked on his fear of rejection and used the mental oasis to solve his problems. One by one he eliminated all the excuses that were getting in the way.

The conclusion that Tom reached was that while his girlfriend's rejection would prevent him achieving his goal in this relationship, he was getting in the way of his own goal by not asking the dreaded question. Finally, Tom realised that if he did nothing, the problem would remain.

The right solution is by no means the easiest. But at least it allows you to move forward and not be stuck with the same problem. Eventually, Tom asked his girlfriend to marry him.

I couldn't help smiling when Tom called me to share his good news. 'She said yes, she said yes!' he burbled ecstatically. 'And you'll love this one, Eileen – she said she was beginning to think I'd never ask because I had a commitment problem.'

I can't promise you a happy ever after ending like that one. But if you keep making excuses I guess you'll never know.

Tom's behaviour was typical of what I call self-sabotage. Sabotaging your own goals is an all too common phenomenon, which is why you need to eliminate as many excuses as possible to determine what's really holding you back.

Going back to the previous exercise, read your goals again and work on eliminating any answers involving other people. It's tricky, I know, but unless you constantly bring the goal back to yourself the responsibility of achieving it lies with someone else. Here are some more examples:

- **Health goal:** To lose weight.

- **Excuse:** My boss insists on me taking clients out to dinner.

- **Financial goal:** Save more money.

- **Excuse:** My partner overspends.

- **Family/extended family:** Have more time to myself

- **Excuse:** My family makes so many demands on me.

Making it somebody else's fault lets you off the hook. Put blame to one side and it's not so tempting to come up with excuses. The issue of being overweight is neither the boss's fault nor the problem. A partner's overspending can be tackled, even if it involves issues over access to joint finances or even examining the breakdown in communication within that relationship. Family life certainly makes demands on time, but ultimately personal choices are made about delegating time.

▪ Short-Circuiting Your Goals

In electrical terms, a short circuit deflects a current through a path of low resistance. You can see how the same analogy applies to goals. To pursue your current path you can opt for one with maximum or minimum resistance. To go for the easy option all the time is a fast way to lose sight of your goal. There's nothing wrong with a bit of re-routeing on the way. But some challenges have to be faced head on.

If you want the beginner's guide to creating lots of short circuits, find as many excuses as possible. If you are good at finding excuses, try putting some of that creative ability into finding solutions. The results are much more rewarding.

Short-circuiting can cause you to get caught up with the incidentals. Your train of thought becomes distracted and you go off on a tangent. Teresa, a client of mine, came to me for coaching to deal with the problem of being let down by a friend and to regain her motivation for starting her own business.

A friend had promised to go into partnership with her and Teresa welcomed the added support of a joint venture. A few weeks later, without warning, the friend pulled out.

By the time she came to see me, she had spent a month discussing the situation with friends and family. 'I've gone over it again and again in my mind,' she'd say, 'and I still don't know what went wrong. One minute my friend was as keen as mustard, then she changed her mind without so much as a thought for me.'

It all sounded a bit odd until, after some more discussion, it emerged that, originally, Teresa had planned to go it alone anyway.

Her goal did not involve the co-operation of a second party, and her friend was merely an accident that had happened along the way. Nevertheless, Teresa experienced a major setback. 'It's hardly surprising that I've lost my motivation when things like that happen,' she said. 'Can you tell me how to get it back?'

This was where I upped the coaching pace by saying: 'Well it would help if you stopped blaming your friend.' Teresa was taken aback. After all, everyone else agreed with her that her friend had behaved badly. This may well have been the case, but it wasn't moving Teresa forward. Associating blame will keep you stuck with the problem, and my aim was to coach Teresa past this block.

After some discussion, Teresa agreed to spend the following week working on her goal. She could also see the advantage of not keeping the focus on the situation that had occurred with her friend, or of using the situation as an excuse for not staying on track with her goal. The following week, Teresa was back on course, with motivation redoubled. By her own admittance, it had made a huge difference for her not to have pursued the same line of thought that had kept her blocked.

Support from all sides is always welcome, but when friends or family support your negative emotions, it may keep you blocked with an excuse. By all means allow yourself to deal with upset and disappointment. Seek support when you need it, and look for balance to keep things in perspective. But when you are dealing with a difficult situation, if everyone around you is contributing the same feedback, your balance will suffer. Stay on track by reminding yourself what that goal is. However disturbing and unwelcome an interruption is, make a conscious effort to stay focused by contributing to your goals on a daily basis. Don't lose sight of them.

▪ Filling in the Blanks

In the previous chapter, I discussed how the brain is always predicting future events. I learned about this from a colleague of mine called Andrew Walton, who is a consultant psychologist. Andrew introduced me to a book called *The Psychology of Personal Constructs*, written some forty years ago by the American psychologist

George Kelly. Kelly's fundamental theory was that a person's thinking processes were governed by how they *anticipated* events.

One of Andrew's roles as a psychologist is to help people overcome their fear of flying. His clients include Air 2000, the flying arm of First Choice Holidays. Andrew's policy is entitled: 'Never leave anything to the imagination'. By that he's referring to the imagination of fearful passengers. Andrew's techniques are so good that by the end of his course, clients are persuaded to embark on a maiden flight.

What Andrew does is fill in the missing blanks. The tendency we have when we don't know the answer is to fill the gap with what we think *must be* the answer. Fear is more inclined to seek out both a false and negative answer. So when the aircraft is rolling down the runway and passengers hear bumping wheels, they are reassured that cats' eyes or concrete strips on the tarmac are generating the sound. This alleviates the concern experienced by some passengers that the aircraft's wheels are falling off the axle. Equally, when the aircraft takes off, passengers are told that the rumbling sound is the undercarriage being retracted, not the engine falling out.

Andrew's clients are taught to recognise that fear persuades people to predict the worst possible outcome. What impressed me so much about his techniques is the fact that clients can apply them to other areas of their life.

In order to succeed you have to remain positive. This becomes difficult when your point of reference is blurry or clouded by negative memories. Information is the key to creating an association.

The brain has access to past and present information to anticipate a future event, but it also likes to predict future information. To give you an example, you may have a goal to run your own business. Existing memory banks tell you that you have no experience in the field of accountancy and cannot afford to bring in a bookkeeper. This could be seen as a good excuse not to pursue that goal. On the other hand you might have signed up for a bookkeeping course and thereby eliminated a prediction for future failure.

Every time you make an excuse for not pursuing a particular goal you are filling in the missing blanks with negative anticipation. Whether you have gone down that road before or are visiting it for the first time, the association has to be positive. This is where you can further your development skills, so for example if your goal is to get a new job, you would want to gather as much information as possible about the vacancy before the interview. You may be required to brush up on existing skills or learn a few new skills in order to be the most suitable candidate. The more information you have, the better, as this can steer you away from repeating past experiences and prevent you from falling foul of undesirable future ones.

▪ Make Your Goal Real

Now for a bit of practical application: read your goals daily to keep your brain on alert mode. When the goal is at the forefront of your mind, useful information or opportunities are less likely to escape your attention. So, if you have reminded yourself that before too long you plan to join a gym, and a leaflet from the local health club happens to arrive through the post, put it in your file. If you have been wondering about signing up with a savings or pension scheme, there could be some useful information in the newspaper that day. Cut it out and stick it in your file. Review the contributions you have made to your file on a weekly basis. If any areas haven't been added to, make a conscious decision to do so the following week.

The more information you gather, the more real the goal becomes. By contributing daily, the goal feels like an integral part of your life, not some distant daydream. Remember that when fear and uncertainty creep in, the missing blanks in your game plan are usually filled with false and negative answers.

▪ The Power of Positive Visualisation

As with any of the techniques discussed in this book, it's not enough to understand them on a purely intellectual level. The only way to benefit is by applying them. Never underestimate the power of positive visualisation. At any given time your brain is predicting the outcome of events. When clients say to me 'Why bother? I'm bound to fail anyway, I always do', I'm inclined to agree with them. With an attitude like that there's no room for success. Actions are governed by thought processes. If failure is what you predict, you should find no problem setting the wheels in motion to achieve just that.

There is no guarantee that success is waiting for you around the next corner. The most successful people experience setbacks, but that's exactly how they see them – as setbacks, not failures. Being positive definitely affects your recovery rate. Do you really know anyone who has never experienced disappointment? Of course not: it's something we all go through. The difference is that the positive person swallows the bitter pill, whereas the negative person scoffs the whole bottle. Obviously it takes far longer to recover from an overdose than just a mouthful of unpleasant medicine.

▪ Upping your Recovery Rate

A fit person, as Roger Black would be able to testify, has a good recovery rate. Their pulse quickly returns to normal when their body is exerted. The same applies to a healthy mind. If you use up all the megabytes in the mental computer it's time to offload. There are only so many thoughts that can be held at one time. When you get stuck in a negative mind-set, the positive thoughts struggle to find a way in.

This final technique is devised to make room for recovery time and throw out those excuses once and for all.

Maybe because of my own experience, I feel it's crucial not to overlook the importance of recognising the symptoms that occur when the body is put under strain. Similar symptoms are experienced when the mind is put under strain. Look at panic attacks. Any victim will tell you that they felt like they were dying: their heart was racing, bursting out of their chest, shaking was common, sweating, breathlessness, an overwhelming feeling of fear. It's a terrifying experience.

To treat any symptom you must first recognise the warning signals. You may recall me saying in Chapter 3 that positive mental thinking is not a means to anaesthetise your emotions. We are emotional beings and subject to a whole range of feelings. What the brain refuses to acknowledge the body will take on board. This isn't as esoteric as it sounds: you only have to look at the reactions that occur in your own body to link the two. When the right person phones, your heart starts racing. When they don't, there's a hollow feeling in the pit of your stomach.

The mind can play a big part in getting us over-excited. Calming the thought processes can alleviate the onset of new symptoms and reduce the effects of existing ones. There are also ways to administer a bit of tender loving care when the body cries out for it. Parents comfort a crying child with soothing words and actions. They create both a mental and physical oasis. Combining the two produces the best results.

Recalling your mental oasis, the advantage of this technique is that you have allocated time to deal with a problem. Unless an urgent decision is required, the brain quickly accepts the new routine of thinking and dealing with problems at the appropriate time. This gives you mental breathing space. The important factor is to recognise the reactions and signals given off by your body, and treat them. Clients have often followed this philosophy and found ways to deal with their own symptoms.

Jack, who works in the city, got a phone call at work from his girlfriend to tell him she didn't want to see him again. With ten minutes to go before a major presentation he had to act quickly. He alerted his secretary that he would be in conference for the next ten minutes and put his phone on voice mail. Knowing he would not be disturbed, Jack lay on the floor of his office and focused on his breathing. Mentally he would deal with the problem when he got home. But he could not afford to go into the presentation a quivering wreck. By the time Jack gave the presentation he had alleviated his breathless condition.

Hillary was shocked when the bathroom ceiling in her new flat collapsed a week after she had moved in. On viewing the extent of the damage she called a friend and asked to borrow her bathroom for an hour. When the friend agreed, Hillary jumped into her car armed with a bag full of pampering goodies. When Hillary emerged from her friend's bathroom, freshly exfoliated, smothered in body lotion and reeking of French perfume, she felt much more able to deal with the disaster.

And on the theme of bathrooms there's one story I can't resist telling you. I was having an office renovated. Late one evening I decided to look in and see how the builders had got on that day. They had made good progress and I was just about to leave when I heard a noise on the top floor. Going upstairs to investigate, one of the builders emerged from the bathroom. 'Hope you don't mind,' he said, 'but I've had a really stressful day and I needed a good soak. Don't worry, I've left it all tidy.' And with that he went whistling past me. On that occasion his recovery rate was clearly better than mine!

▪ Conclusion

- ► Successful people have the right attitude. They don't look for excuses to fail.

- ► It's up to you to achieve your goals. Don't make other people your excuse.

- ► Push beyond the excuse and find the real reason that's holding you back.

- ► Goals can mean you stepping into new territory. Recognise that excuses are part of the fear process.

- ► Fill in the missing blanks. Don't let your imagination run away with you. Gather information and increase your development skills. Then you can make an informed choice.

- ► Up your recovery rate. Work on creating a mental and physical oasis.

- ► Read your goals daily. For a goal to be achievable it needs mental attention. Keep it in mind – your thoughts influence your actions.

- ► Review your file weekly and make sure you are contributing to all seven areas.

- ► Allocate a time frame for achieving your goals.

CHAPTER SIX

Time Management and Making the Right Decision

I F YOU WANT TO MAKE changes in your life, you have to create the space to do it. And if you're serious about those changes, you will find yourself involved in clearing space on many levels, so this chapter will cover both physical and mental clearing. Much, though not all, of this process is to do with how you manage your own time. Time affects the decisions you make, so it's important to look at how you prioritise your time, or set aside time to make decisions. You also need to find out whether you are caught up in the past or are able to embrace the future, allowing time for your goals and providing the time to bring into your life what you truly desire.

There will also be techniques to improve your ability to manage your time and get the best from it. You wouldn't want to clear out the spare bedroom, only to fill it with the same things again. The same applies to mental space clearing. You won't gain anything by cluttering up your mind with the same old thoughts or unrealistic demands.

I tell you this because I know how easy it is to gather things and how hard it is to let them go. But letting go can be very liberating. What did it for me was that I had made the decision to walk a different path. That, and the fact that following major spinal surgery my physiotherapist had banned me from wearing many of the fashionable but entirely unpractical footwear in my collection. Not that I've entirely converted to sensible walking shoes, but there is a greater need to remain practical. Possessions can remain an extension of your personality without being a useless accessory. When you decide to bring new things into your life there is no need to hold on to many of the old things.

Here is a summary of the areas you'll be covering in this chapter.

- Filling a box. How to be selective about the possessions you keep.

- Clearing your surroundings so that the past doesn't get in the way of the present or the future.

- Making some mental space.

- Time management.

- Techniques for making effective decisions.

If you are an extremely tidy person, the first part of this chapter will be a useful reminder of the areas that need attention. If, on the other hand, you are like the vast majority of the population, your drawers are probably crammed to bursting point, and your wardrobes will be stuffed full. So let's get cracking.

▪ Creating Space

1. **Allocate time** First, you need to allocate some time for this project and stick to it. However much time you decide to put aside, take my advice and treble it. Jobs like this don't take twice as long as you think: they usually take three times as long. And this is one task that you can't afford to leave half-finished.

2. **Preparation** We all know that what's excess to one person may prove useful to another, but in truth, most of us find it hard to throw things out, so a better alternative is to put them to a different use or let someone else benefit from them. Find out where your nearest clothes banks are, along with recycling centres, charity shops, second-hand shops, car boot sales, jumble sales and charity organisations. I also suggest you stock up with some strong bin bags or boxes. Forget storage containers for the time being. This exercise is

not one for neatly storing or tidying away what you have already gathered. It's out with the old, and in with the new. Time to let go.

3. **Where to begin** Tidiness, like charity, begins at home so let's make that our priority. There's no point in starting on the surface and clearing away obvious and visible mess. The one rule that applies to a mass clear out is that once you start, everything gets a whole lot messier at first. To make things easier, I suggest that you take a room at a time. Allocate an area in the house as the central depot or collection point. The hallway would be very suitable as it's close to the door and the best place for things that are on the way out.

Begin by attacking the drawers, cupboards and wardrobes, and then move on to shelves, nooks and crannies and any other space you are inclined to fill. Here are your options for what you do with the piles of stuff you unload: put it back, move it, or dispose of it. Take care with the first two options. There are no points for putting everything back neatly or finding a less obvious hiding place. The objective is to remove what you no longer need. 'But what if I need it in the future?' you might be saying. Well, unless you know for sure that you do and you've got room to create a museum of the past there is no strong case for holding on to it. If something holds a strong sentimental value ask yourself the following questions. Is the memory a good one or bad one? Is it keeping my attention in the past and stopping me moving forward? How would it affect me if I no longer had this possession?

There is a technique I often use with clients called 'Fill a box', in which I ask clients who are struggling to space-clear to fill a box with the possessions they would like to salvage from a fire. It sounds a bit dramatic, I know. But knowing people who have at some time in their life lost every possession they had, I was left with a greater insight into what is truly valuable.

Imagine you could only keep a box full of items from each room you've cleared. You'll soon see how it affects your selection process. Once you have placed any items of real value in a box it's a lot easier to deal with what's left. When it comes to getting rid of clothes, separate them out into seasons. Then you can start to reduce each pile. If you didn't wear something last season, are you likely to wear it next season?

> Isabel was called home from work unexpectedly. Her house was on fire. Luckily, there was no one at home and her family was safe, and the insurance would cover the damage, but Isabel still had to contend with the loss. She told me: 'As I raked through the ashes there were so few things that I really hoped had survived. Every time I stumbled on something of true value my heart skipped a beat.' Isabel was only able to retrieve a box full of items.

Life, of course, is never stationary and time refuses to stand still. Just as you can get caught up with unhappy memories that keep you blocked, happy ones can also get in the way. When clients bring a whole host of experiences with them, time is the key factor. Fear of painful memories can keep you blocked from embracing change and wanting to freeze a moment in time can also keep you blocked.

I'm sure there have been times when a conversation with a friend has caused you to conclude that they are locked in the past, reliving an experience either mentally or emotionally. Whether that experience is good or bad, you are bound to want to move them forward, but when that stuck person is you, the way out is harder to find. You can't see what's in front of you if you are always looking back. Allowing yourself to let go is the best test. So here's what you do. Look around your home: are you building a shrine or a sanctuary?

As human beings, our survival instincts supply the basics: food, warmth and shelter. Progressing beyond these you invest time in creating your shelter. Comfort is often a high priority. You mark out your territory in a manner that reflects both your needs and mood. But sometimes that happens on a subconscious level. Your environment may start off cheerful and yet something happens along the way. You can store it both mentally and physically. A physical clear-out is a great way for you to proceed to a mental clear-out.

Clive had fond memories of his days at university. In fact his flat was a shrine to the past. Photographs covered his walls. There was the beer run to Belgium, a riotous pyjama party, a weekend camping holiday in Cornwall, tickets from a Gary Numan concert and a picture of an ex-girlfriend by his bedside. Yes, Clive had fond memories and every day he relived them. The only problem was that life seemed so much less fun these days. How Clive longed to be that carefree student again.

During the week, Clive looked the part in his city business suit. At weekends he looked the archetypal student and reverted to a wardrobe that had seen better days. When old friends used to visit, the same comments always emerged. 'Oh Clive, you haven't changed a bit . . .' 'Are you never going to get a new wardrobe . . .?' and so on. On the other hand, they *had* changed. Clive felt dismayed. His new situation felt unfamiliar and he could no longer capture the atmosphere of the past with old friends.

Clive went along with my suggestion to give his flat a major overhaul, but at first I didn't feel I could ask Clive to junk all his beloved memorabilia, so instead I asked him to remove it from sight for a while. I still find it difficult to contain my excitement at the difference it made. There are some case histories that stick out in my mind. Clive is one of them. At our next weekly session you couldn't miss the upbeat tone in his voice. I was introduced to a whole set of new people. Clive talked about the people he worked with, how funny the woman in the cafeteria was who liked to call him the 'main man', how his secretary was addicted to soaps on TV and how he had signed up for a t'ai chi course every Monday for fifteen weeks.

The following week, Clive told me that he had thrown out most of the contents of his flat. Now he was busy redecorating, changing colour schemes, buying new furniture and planning a dinner party for a few friends from work. He had so dreaded letting go, but once he had done it, it was easy to fill the space with something new.

Waking up every day to familiar surroundings can cause you to become visually immune. That's not to say you aren't feeling the effects on many other levels. Once Clive had got over the initial hurdle, he was able to make changes on many levels without my asking him to do so. When the physical blocks were removed his reactions became spontaneous.

Why not enlist the help of a friend? You might be missing something that they see immediately. It took my sister to point out that my own home contained some trophies to my past. And that was just where they kept me. I'm not suggesting you eliminate every memory of the past, only the ones that stop you embracing the present. A client told me how a friend helped her to transform her kitchen. She had always loved to cook. But when her children left home, cooking for her husband and herself became an unwelcome chore. The kitchen had previously been a family place, filled with noise and laughter. The notice board was covered with family recipes as was the bookshelf. What could ever replace that loving atmosphere?

In fact, just by making a few simple changes, my client was able to recapture her love of cooking. The recipes on the notice board changed, as did the books to Meals for Two. The shopping list had a new priority. Previously my client had wandered around the supermarket putting things in the trolley only to have her husband remind her they were no longer feeding an army and didn't need the family pack. Now she made a list in advance and planned ahead. The new list was practical and stopped the painful knee-jerk reminders.

Summary

► If you want to hold on to memories, use your journal to write them down. You can re-visit your diary whenever you feel the need.

► You don't have to surround yourself with a map of your life to date.

► Plan ahead. Use your file to invest in some new experiences. If you want your future to look exciting, make it look exciting on paper.

► Don't underestimate the impact your surroundings have. They can stimulate your last thought at night and your first thought in the morning.

▪ Keeping the Mind Healthy

Contrary to the popular belief that memory declines with age, we now know that under normal circumstances the brain has an enormous facility to store memory. But to develop this, it's important to keep feeding the brain new information, e.g. by learning new skills, stretching your mental capacities with brain-teasers and playing word games, as well as doing crosswords and other memory-enhancing exercises. Without this ongoing mental stimulation, the memory banks can become jumbled. We've talked about putting things in their place on a practical level, but to have mental clarity the brain has to be kept busy and active. When the memory banks are functioning efficiently, you can allocate mental space which allows you to apply all your mental resources to a particular problem or situation. In order to create mental space, the brain has to remain full, as opposed to empty.

Mental Space Clearing

The first stage of mental space clearing is developing a healthy mind and then prioritising your thought processes. Just as it's important to prioritise time, you also need to prioritise your thoughts in an orderly fashion. Healthy minds have a better ability to concentrate and focus when you are dealing with the situations that life throws at you. It helps when you can keep your attention on one thing at a time, so if you have a problem at work that requires a lot of mental application, you will find it a lot more difficult to solve if you are thinking about what time you've got to pick up the kids, what you're having for dinner that evening, whether you've paid the phone bill and so on. The important thing is that time management doesn't just involve what you do with your time, it also has a lot to do with what you do with your mind during that time.

▪ Time Management

Time is not some mysterious phenomenon that plays ball for some players and refuses to co-operate with others. Why is it that some individuals are able to achieve so much? Richard Branson doesn't have more hours in the day than you do. The 'lady who lunches' who is always late for appointments doesn't have fewer. There are certainly many practical applications that you can use to produce immediate results, but only if you are prepared to take responsibility for administering them. Your own time is relative to you. Others make demands on it, at times impose on it and even invade it, but ultimately only you can truly delegate it.

Separate your short-term goals from your long-term ones. To keep things simple, keep short-term goals as goals you wish to achieve within a three-month period, and view your long-term goals as any you will achieve thereafter. Next to each goal write a date for achieving that goal. To confirm your commitments, write the date in your diary and/or calendar: your mental preparation is under way. All you have to do now is make the time to follow through with the practical application.

Trying to fit goals into an already overloaded schedule will not produce the results you desire. Of course, you can get a couple more hours out of the day by getting up an hour earlier and going to bed an hour later. You can also add to the statistics of a culture that is showing many of the symptoms of information overload. With greater access to information than ever before there's increasing pressure to cram the mental data banks. The result is overload. Many individuals ignore the cause of the condition and look to time management gurus to relieve their symptoms. Worse still, you may be looking for techniques to enable you to do more, but not being selective about how you fill your time can have detrimental consequences. At one end of the scale there is the lack of fulfilment and apathy that sets in from not pursuing the life you desire, and at the other end of the scale there is a fatigued, overworked and overwhelmed individual. Both situations cause stress.

When Sarah came to me for coaching, she was clearly overloaded and exhausted with her daily schedule. Sarah was a working mum, and her day started at seven when the kids woke up. After that, there was the school run followed by the nursery run, then a quick dash to her invalid mother to get her up and organised for the morning. Then she would collect her youngest daughter at lunchtime, followed by a never-ending round of housework. Sarah's pace was relentless. Even in the evening, she was working on her husband's bookkeeping before she collapsed into bed exhausted.

Coaching helped Sarah to see that this was an impossible schedule for anyone to keep up. Much as she felt that her responsibility was to look after her mother as well as her husband and children, she was pushing herself so hard that she was in danger of collapsing with exhaustion. Once Sarah realised that she was asking too much of herself, she found it much easier to ask for help. Finding a carer for her mother relieved a lot of the pressure that Sarah was under, while still allowing her to visit on a daily basis. As you can see in Sarah's case, she needed to offload some of the demands being made of her, rather than use time management to create more space in an already over-loaded day.

Prioritising Your Priorities

When you have decided what you really want, you can plan accordingly. Start by making a list of how your week pans out.

► Only include what takes place in an average week

► Don't include in the list things you intend to do, but rarely get round to doing.

Try using this as a guideline:

► **Preparation time** This includes time spent getting up, dressing, undressing, shaving, applying make-up, doing your hair, using the bathroom, cleaning, cooking, washing the car, doing the school run, shopping, doing the laundry, ironing, commuting and sitting in traffic, queuing up.

► **Working time** How many hours you spend each day working.

► **Recreation time** Include watching television, playing sport, going to the gym, gardening, DIY, walking the dog, socialising with friends, family, your partner – generally anything you consider to be a recreational pursuit.

► **Development time** Give some thought to this category as it includes anything that you see as a means of personal development. It may be mental, spiritual and physical. So you can include study time, reading, learning a new skill, meditating, praying.

► **Time out** This is the time when you do nothing – and I mean nothing. No television, music, stimulation, conversation or company. This is time spent alone, so only fill in this category if you are in the habit of setting aside time to do absolutely nothing.

► **Pampering time** There may be a few things that you consider to be pampering. But, as a tip, only include things that you have made a conscious effort to include in your week. So, for example, if the kids go to bed early one night and you manage to fit in a relaxing bath don't include that. On the other hand, if you have booked a massage for yourself or pre-planned a treat, include that.

This list is designed to keep things simple. You may need to time yourself for a week to find out how much time is spent in each area. You may even come up with a few more areas you want to include. The objective is to find out just what you are doing with your time. If you don't know, how can you plan ahead?

Once you know what you are doing with your time you can decide what you actually want to do with it. The response I often get from clients is: 'Well, if it was that easy I'd already be doing it.' For some reason there is often an assumption that doing what you want with your time only involves doing things you like. The choice factor gets overlooked. So let's get back to payback for a minute. The time you invest produces a result. You may not like the task very much, but the result is desirable. Therefore you choose to do it. Review your weekly list: how many things on it can you say that you were forced to do? Be honest: there may well be consequences for not doing them, but can you really say you had no choice in the matter?

The issue of time seems to cause the greatest dilemma with people who refuse to accept any responsibility for how they delegate it, preferring to claim that other people control their time. Unless you are being held prisoner against your own will, is there really any substantial argument that others govern your time?

I'm keen to hear a case against what I've just said. So I'd like you to put your best case forward. In your journal, I'd like you to list all the reasons why you have little or no control over your time.

When you've done that, it's time to put on your coach's hat as you are about to overcome a major challenge. Something is getting in the way of your time management. What you need to find out is if you are the major culprit. Apply the techniques from Chapter 5 – No More Excuses. You should by now have a list of reasons of all the things that interfere with your time management. By eliminating excuses you can get to the source of the block.

The purpose of this exercise is to see if you can eliminate yourself from the equation. This means that you have no choice in the matter at any time. To overcome any problems listed, imagine you are playing a videotape. You can rewind, pause, stop or fast forward. Here's an example:

> John was head-hunted from his previous job and was working in the city as a fund manager. At the interview he was fully briefed on exactly what was expected from him, but the rewards were high, and included an attractive salary and generous bonus scheme. John and his wife discussed the implications of the move and both agreed the offer was too good to refuse. A choice was made. John and his wife were now experiencing the consequences of that choice.
>
> John worked long hours and was expected to be available day or night when required. This was affecting his family life. His wife and children hardly saw him and when they did he was tired and bad-tempered. John came to see me because he felt that he had no control over the time and hours he was expected to work.
>
> John was looking for a way to balance his life around a working day that could stretch out to fifteen hours.
>
> John realised that he did have a choice in the matter. After all, it had been his decision in the first place to take a job that involved such long working hours. The culture of the company was such that they made no allowances for family or even social life. Rightly or wrongly, that was the company policy and, while acceptable to many, John felt that his true values were being compromised. In order for John to achieve the desired balance in his life, he made

the decision to look for a job with more flexible working hours. John is much happier in his new job. While he has taken a substantial drop in salary, he values the time he gets to spend with his wife and children.

If work was your top priority then possibly you could accommodate such a schedule. But if there were other priorities, how much do you think you could fit in between those working hours? You may find that the financial rewards more than compensate for the demands made on your time. This may allow your partner to stay home with your children, buy the house you have always dreamed of and enjoy luxury holidays. John's priorities were different; he would not be able to embrace these values and juggle his time satisfactorily. So, we're back to values.

Time is valuable, indeed precious. If you want to be around for your children, you can't rewind the tape and make up for lost time. You can try compensating, but you can't recapture a time gone by. So, to help you prioritise your time, look at your values. Remind yourself of what's important to you. This will help you to make the right choice. John valued his marriage and children. He resented the hours spent working because they took him away from the people he loved. In hindsight it was easy for John to see that time was not so much the issue as the choices he had made to take the job in the first place. But making the right decision is not easy. Have your values paramount in your mind before you make a decision that will influence the demands made of your time and the consequences it will have on your life.

Here is an immensely useful extract from a book called *The Perfect Decision*. It's by Andrew Leigh, a senior partner at Maynard Leigh, a company that specialises in 'Unlocking People Potential'.

Ten Decision Life-Savers

1. Beware of over-reliance on instinct

Gut feelings suggest we know the right choice to make. Instinct is usually best used, though, when you have plenty of facts and information. Some decisions are 'counter intuitive'.

2. Write it down

Since many decisions involve juggling with lots of facts and feelings, making sense of them in your head can be difficult, if not impossible. Writing down the information in some systematic way, such as the pros and cons, may improve your handling of some choices.

3. Stress warps judgement

Strong feelings or potentially serious consequences can seriously distort decision-making. Find ways to reduce stress through, for example, talking about the choice with someone else, allowing more time for deliberation or adopting relaxation methods such as breathing deeply several times to calm you at the point of decision.

4. Clarify time scale

Many choices do not require an immediate decision. You frequently have time to allow more information to be accumulated before deciding. It is not being decisive to rush into a choice when more reflection or information might produce a better result.

5. Simple statistics improve some choices

We rarely know the full consequences of a decision. So most choices are based on our guess about the probabilities – the chance of something occurring. The human desire to make sense of things and see patterns where perhaps none exist can lead one astray. Simple statistical methods can aid many decisions.

6. Use your brain

It helps to sleep on a difficult decision before arriving at your final choice. Your brain is like a computer, able to sift complex facts and judgements without your conscious state interfering. You will often wake up next day, clear about what to do.

7. Employ available information

Look for information that might contradict your point of view. Refusal to seek evidence that might show one is wrong is a common cause of poor decisions. If choice has cost you a great deal of time and money it can be very tempting to stick with it, even though the evidence suggests this is a wrong decision.

8. The past is a poor indicator

We cannot know the future which, by definition, has not yet happened. It is therefore tempting to rely on the past to tell us what the future holds. Because something has happened even many times before does not necessarily mean it will automatically occur again.

9. Keep money in perspective

Reducing all decisions to a question of money is misguided, even if you are an accountant or treasury official. Many choices involve consequences that are not readily or appropriately reduced to money terms.

10. Make it your choice

A group may become so committed to a choice that it unconsciously combines to reject anything that contradicts what it wants to do. Similarly, an authority figure can sometimes influence decisions inappropriately, when more objective reasoning would suggest a different choice. Make sure when you make a choice that it is yours and not someone else's.

Take the time to read through this list when you are making an important decision. (Why not copy out this list into your file for easy reference?) Bear in mind that just as decisions influence your time, time will also influence your decisions.

If, for example, taking a particular job seems like the right decision at the time, you have to make sure that you are weighing up all the pros and cons. Your work situation can influence other areas of your life, so it's not enough to weigh up one job in relation to another one. Perhaps because we like to place things in a particular category, the comparison is like for like. You may not be giving enough thought to the demands made on your time, how the job affects family life, the levels of stress that are incurred, the overall job satisfaction and how you will maintain a balance with the other vitally important areas of your life.

Work takes up a major part of most people's day. Not every aspect of your working life may be entirely to your satisfaction, but if there are more minuses than pluses, a large part of your day is being spent somewhere you don't want to be. When problems occur in one area of your life, few have the ability to separate them from other areas. They have a habit of leaking out, especially when they dominate time.

You would think that a lot of emphasis would be given to the aspect of quality time. Yet it rarely is. How many people hold on to relationships well after their sell-by date, continue to maintain the company of people they don't particularly like and constantly battle to overcome the biggest culprit of mismanaged time – procrastination.

Procrastination seems to take a strong hold when the major part of your day feels compromised. You are stuck doing things you don't want to do. Maintaining a balance will keep procrastination at bay. There will always be a certain amount of time spent doing less enjoyable tasks. However these tasks can be achieved with minimum discomfort when you feel you have some choice in the matter. So be aware of the decisions you make which have conse-quences and which will influence the running order of your day.

▪ Conclusion

- ► Make a list of how your average week pans out.

- ► Set aside the necessary time to achieve goals. Decide what changes you want to make, i.e. what stays and what goes.

- ► Refer to your values. Your time will feel compromised when your values are.

- ► Use the Ten Decision Life-Savers.

- ► If you are constantly battling with the issue of time, find out what possible excuses are preventing you from coming out the winner.

- ► Finding time requires forward planning. If you want to achieve your goals, don't expect time to appear miraculously – you have to make it.

CHAPTER SEVEN

Communication Skills

I F YOU WANT TO relate to others by building successful relationships it is essential that you learn to compromise and negotiate effectively, whether in social or professional relationships. It is my aim in this chapter to develop the techniques which you should find equally beneficial in either case. I have deliberately positioned this chapter at the end of the first half of this book, because it is so crucial. It is no use mastering the other techniques if you can't go on to communicate them effectively.

Taking a single-minded approach is useful to narrow your focus, determine your values and strengthen your sense of purpose. But that approach is no good if you exclude other people from your game plan. Of course there are people who go through life cutting down everything that stands in their way, but they leave a pretty sorry mess behind them. I prefer to adopt an approach that's based on consideration and courtesy. You need to be able to communicate effectively in order to achieve your goals.

There is a common misunderstanding I regularly encounter in coaching, that in order to get what you want you have to be ruthless, but it is by no means a prerequisite for achieving goals. When you identify successful people it's only natural to pick out character traits. They possess a sense of purpose, a driving energy, a degree of single-mindedness and ambition. Some are ruthless, there is no denying it, but many are not. And you'd be surprised at how many have got their way by compromising. A factory boss who refused to allow her workers to take more than a ten-minute tea break found that not only were her staff disgruntled, but also the quality control department were rejecting more and more items. Recognising that the staff were clearly unhappy, the boss compromised by extending their breaks. Within a few weeks, not only had the productivity increased but the quality of the goods had improved too.

The word compromise means different things to different people. To help you in reading this chapter, I'd like you to list in your journal an image that the word 'compromise' throws up for you. If you associate compromise with putting yourself or another person in a dishonourable position – being compromised – you could say that this has negative connotations. However, it's important to relate positively to the word 'compromise' and see that there are benefits in a half-way house. You are far more likely to reach an agreement and avoid conflict when both parties head for the middle ground. In order to negotiate effectively you have to relate positively to the word compromise and recognise it as a position of strength.

If you always seek to win the game and point score on your own terms, there is no room for team effort. Compromise paves the way to successful relationships on every level.

▪ Fine-Tuning Your Communication Skills

You have the potential to be an excellent communicator. After all, you have been practising from an early age! Somewhere along the way, though, that ability may have become suppressed. A dogmatic parent can suppress a child's ability to communicate, as can an overly critical teacher or a bullying boss. They lead to your giving out mixed signals which detract from your natural spontaneity. Good communicators act naturally: there are no mixed signals in the messages they relay and their sincerity is apparent. Regardless of your present level of skill in this area, the good news is that you can make rapid progress developing communication, with immediate results!

Which qualities would you associate with that of being a good communicator? I expect we could all come up with a few – the ability to listen, to relay information clearly and precisely, and to present and respond to ideas with enthusiasm. But there's one quality that is often overlooked: consideration. The effective communicator always extends consideration to the listener and audience. Even when they want to get a point across they provide space for consideration. This can take the form of limiting talk time so that the listener can respond and give feedback, or ensuring that written correspondence is as clear as it can possibly be.

How many times have you received a letter and wanted to throw it in the bin immediately? The next time you do, think about why it didn't hold your attention. Perhaps it was full of jargon, or was irrelevant to your needs, or perhaps it reeked of insincerity. This is a useful exercise because it helps you to identify what caused you to disregard the message. Being aware of ineffectual communication can steer you away from using it. Equally, when something gets your attention, make a note of why. Do the same thing with verbal communication.

Use your journal to list the things that make you a good communicator as compared to a bad one. It may help you to think of people you know, such as a friend who is a great storyteller and can hold a captive audience, or the all-time bore who constantly interrupts and talks over everyone. Once you establish the traits which make an effective communicator, you will be in a better position to negotiate with people in order to fulfil your goals and to work through any problems.

Bad Communicators

Don't fall into the trap of repeating ineffectual modes of communication. Here are just a few examples of what to avoid.

▶ **Jargon** There is nothing clever about using convoluted jargon and it rarely impresses anyone other than the person using it. You may think it makes you sound intelligent, but the truly wise prefer to get their message across. They use a language that is appropriate to the listener and audience. What's clever about having a conversation when no one knows what you're talking about? The only thing it demonstrates is ignorance – ignorance of the fact that your message is going unheard.

▶ **Hogging the limelight** You know the type, we've all met them, they rarely pause for breath. Their conversations are long monologues with little to define one topic from the next, probably because the majority of the conversation revolves around them. They provide no room for feedback in what amounts to a one-way conversation. I remember being present when a journalist attempted to interview an associate of mine. His first question was immediately met with a machine-gun response that seemed to last for about half an hour. At one point the journalist turned to me and whispered: 'I'm going to fake my own death in a minute.' The moral is – hold fire!

▶ **The interrupter** You can be in the middle of talking and the interrupter cuts right across you. We all have something important to say, but what *they* have to say is far more important. Their bad manners make bad company. It's irritating enough on a social level; immensely frustrating when someone pulls rank to dominate a conversation on a professional level. My method of dealing with interrupters is to keep talking. Simply continue with what you were saying in a relaxed manner and they'll soon get the message. If you are inclined to interrupt, contain your excitement for a little longer and wait for the other person to draw breath – there's your chance!

▶ **Tactlessness** You couldn't miss this type if you tried. They are prone to making remarks like: 'I don't care what people think...' (which is just as well, given the impression they leave) and 'I always speak my mind'. Speaking your mind is not necessarily a bad thing. It just depends on what is in your mind at the time.

Here's a scene I witnessed a few years ago while attending a gala dinner.

I was standing around having a drink with a group of people before the meal began. Most of us were meeting for the first time and exchanging polite chit-chat. A woman in a bright pink fuchsia suit joined our group. She had it all – a combination of stealing the limelight, interrupting and making the most tactless remarks imaginable. Most of us bit our lips and prayed for an early dinner call. When she'd finally insulted the group one by one, she turned her attention to someone who had seemed a very reserved man standing next to me. 'And what is it you do?' she enquired. 'I'm a colour analyst,' he replied. 'Oh, whatever next?' she said loudly. 'I suppose you'll be telling me my colours don't blend with my mood this evening.' 'On the contrary,' he said calmly, 'they blend beautifully with your mood. They're bold, brash and overbearing, just like the person wearing them.' As a final accessory to the woman's outfit her face turned a vivid shade of fuchsia pink.

I'm not suggesting that it is appropriate or desirable to turn the tables on the socially inept. A better approach is to imagine what it would be like to be on the receiving end of your own communication. I've yet to meet a so-called straight-talker who welcomes a dose of his or her own medicine. You can be direct and have clarity in your communication without demonstrating rudeness, hogging the conversation and insulting your audience.

Think up some more undesirable traits and write them down in your journal. Listing them makes a stronger impact than just mentally noting them when they occur. If you are recalling a particular person, think about their body language. Were their mannerisms aggressive? Were they prone to turning their back and pushing people out of a conversation or group? Did they invade your space by getting too close? Examine closely what was going on at the time. Communication takes place on many levels and if you are picking up bad vibes, you've got to be aware of all the signals.

Good Communicators

Now let's review our effective means of communication. The good communicator demonstrates the following skills:

▶ **Having the ability to listen** You might be able to hear a pin drop but what are the chances of hearing a clanger dropped in a conversation? When you are too busy thinking about what you want to say, the chances are you will only receive a fraction of the information being relayed, so slow down, calm your thoughts and concentrate on what the person is saying. Good listeners digest what they have heard before interjecting their own opinion. They might say things like: 'Would I be right in thinking ...?' or 'Does that mean that you think ...?' If they need further clarity they will ask for it.

▶ **Being non-judgemental** My clients often say how frustrating it is when people won't talk to them. I sympathise with them, but have you ever been taken aback when someone has told you about a conversation they have had with someone that you can't get two words out of? So clearly we find it easier to talk to some people than we do to others.

What creates the comfort factor that allows freedom of expression? Well, asking the right questions certainly helps, along with providing space to let the other person talk. But your response is also crucial to what comes next, so when you jump in with judgemental remarks don't expect to be met with a welcoming response.

Many of the issues or problems you have listed on your forms may be resolved by knowing how to negotiate and compromise in both your business and personal relationships. Learning to listen to the other person's point of view and being non-judgemental may give you insights in how to work through any blocks and achieve your goals.

▶ **Having the ability to deal with criticism** Nobody likes criticism. At best it results in defence and at worst provokes attack. When your conversation leads to silence or confrontation there has clearly been a break-down in communication. Let me give you a few examples. Here you can see three typical responses to judgmental remarks: silence, defence and attack.

Liz was relaying to her mother that she had just split up from her boyfriend. She hoped to get a sympathetic ear but instead her mother reacted by saying: 'Oh darling you're hopeless, you can't seem to keep a man around for more than five minutes.' Liz was silent for a few moments.

When Tim asked his boss for advice on reprimanding a member of staff he was hoping to gain some useful input in his new managerial position and not to be told 'You obviously have a problem with responsibility.' Tim immediately felt defensive.

Michael took the initiative to inform a customer who was placing an order that a particular stock item was temporarily delayed due

> to an air freight strike. He hoped the customer would appreciate
> this advance information, rather than be left to experience an
> unexplained delay. 'What kind of tin-pot company are you any-
> way?' was the ungrateful response. Michael felt inclined to attack
> and tell him: 'You're the rudest customer I've had the misfortune
> of dealing with.'

There are methods of expressing discontent and relaying feelings
without steamrollering the other person. When Liz was relaying
the conversation to her mother about the split with her boyfriend
she clearly wanted a sympathetic listener. Tim sought guidance
from a superior in an area that he was inexperienced in. An effective boss would have recognised his ability to request assistance in
dealing with a sensitive issue. Whilst Michael's customer was
clearly inconvenienced by the delay, there was no real reason to
place the blame with Michael's company. The customer could
have expressed his or her discontent for the delay and acknowledged the advance warning.

If you want to encourage free-flowing communication it is a
good idea to concentrate on expressing your personal feelings. As
a useful tip, you are less likely to criticise if you begin a sentence
with 'I feel...' or 'In my opinion ...' rather than 'You are ...' or 'The
trouble with you is ...'. Keeping your conversation in the first person for the most part prevents you from sounding too critical, so
for example you could say: 'I understand what you are saying, but
I don't agree with it.' The other party may want your agreement
but will hear no personal criticism in your words.

▪ Communication Tips

Eye Contact

When talking to a group of people, switch your eye contact
around each person (if the group is small enough). Alternatively, if
a remark is directed at one person, keep your eye contact with
them until you have finished delivering a particular point. If you
have ever listened to or witnessed an experienced public speaker,
you will have noted that they seem to make eye contact with

everyone in the room. This gives the impression that they are still addressing you. The aim is to talk *to* you, not *at* you.

In a one-on-one situation, maintain eye contact and avoid staring or using a fixed gaze, both of which are unnerving and can give out the wrong signals. Keep your eyes relaxed, don't forget to blink and, by lowering your eyes briefly or deflecting them, make the person feel like they still have your attention. Good eye contact confirms your interest, confidence and sincerity in what you are saying.

I'm sure you can think of occasions when someone was reluctant to make eye contact. What sort of message did they project? Slightly shifty, nervous, insincere, having something to hide? The overriding message given out is that all is not as it seems. The listener is distracted from the message by the signals given out. Communication is received on many levels – the ears and eyes are major receptors in the process. Therefore it is important to communicate your message visually in order to reinforce what you are saying.

Clarity

Effective communicators deliver clear and precise information without rambling on or constantly reiterating points. Although their dialogue can appear spontaneous there is generally a high degree of planning involved. Key points are identified and a conversation or written communication is punctuated by bullet points. Mental and written preparation increases your ability to communicate clearly. Try these techniques.

► Think carefully about what you want to say.

► What is the purpose of your communication?

► Who is your audience and are you using a language that is appropriate (i.e. does the situation call for a formal or informal approach)?

► What is your desired outcome?

► Mentally rehearse your conversation in advance, highlighting the key points. You will be less inclined to waffle and confuse your audience.

► Write key points down. Don't expect your audience to read between the lines or pick up the message intuitively.

► Watch your emotions. Positive emotions like enthusiasm and passion drive a message home and demonstrate conviction. Negative emotions like anger and intolerance can result in conflict.

► Watch the jargon. Unless talking to a professional organisation or an audience that understands the terminology you use, find alternative words that are easily understood. The most powerful messages are often the simplest. Look at adverts – a few words say more.

► Set a limit. Imagine you can only use a few sentences to convey your message. Practise writing it out as it helps to condense your thoughts.

Enthusiasm

There is something wonderfully infectious about enthusiastic people. A friend of mine can make a train journey from London to Brighton sound like the trip of the century. How you relay something has a huge impact on your listener. If you want other people to be excited about your ideas, show that you are too.

Keep Smiling

Facial expressions speak volumes. If you are receptive and comfortable to information you are receiving, respond with a smile. When you want the mood to be upbeat, show it with facial expressions. Even when you are talking on the telephone, a smile will influence the inflections in your voice and transfer itself down the line.

Body language

Body language can give away a lot about your mood, so standing with your arms folded can send out a signal that you are being defensive, just as excessive fidgeting will make you appear nervous. The more relaxed you are, the more likely you are to take on a natural stance. Avoid using body language that can be interpreted as being aggressive, e.g. standing too close to someone or using your body to block someone out of a conversation.

▪ How to Negotiate Effectively

You may want to have your point of view heard and be clear about what you have to say, especially in order to accomplish your goals. So, taking some time out to listen to the other person should not present a problem. The problems tend to arise when there is a difference of opinion. Confrontation is not something to go looking for, but it is not always possible to avoid.

The next time a disagreement arises, ask yourself the question: 'Does the other person sound like they believe what they are saying?'. You see, although some individuals are argumentative by nature, most of us feel as passionately about an issue as you do. Opinions matter and that's why many disputes involve both parties fighting to make themselves heard. Are the words 'You're not listening to me' familiar?

So what does it take to make you feel heard?

▶ The other person listens to you, but still disagrees.

▶ The other person meets you half way.

▶ The other person listens to you and agrees with you.

You can see someone's point of view without sharing it. The majority of people locked into a dispute firmly believe they are right. You may well believe you are right, but if you take the attitude that the other person is wrong the dispute continues.

In my capacity as an executive coach working at a senior level with companies, I have often heard the term 'Let's agree to differ'. Despite the regular use of the phrase it rarely moves things on. Individuals still continue to put their case forward. There is in effect no agreement to allow a difference of opinion.

When a team effort is required, as it is in many relationships and certainly within a company structure, an agreement to differ is hardly a useful platform on which to build. A decision needs to be reached. If you enter into any negotiation using a tug-of-war approach the balance will be swayed heavily in one direction. It's better to aim for an agreement to find a compromise than an agreement to differ.

If you really believe an issue is worth making a stand over, ask yourself the following questions:

► Can I achieve what I want without disregarding or overriding the feelings of others?

► Am I prepared to take responsibility for my actions?

► How important is the outcome of the situation to my current and future happiness?

► Does the situation compromise my value system?

► How will the outcome of the situation affect my goals?

To ensure you haven't lost sight of the issue, use the following techniques:

► Keep your focus firmly on your goal and achieving it. Don't get caught up in a personal slanging match.

► Identify the points that both parties agree on. Emphasise these areas and let the other party see there is some common ground.

► When the other party has stated their case, repeat it back to them. Be sure you understand exactly what they are saying and what are the major areas of concern. Ask them to do the same for you. Many disputes involve completely unrelated issues. Be aware just what it is you are disputing.

► Think outside the box. You may only see one outcome or solution. Have you considered alternatives? You'll find it a lot easier to accept your own alternative than see the potential of other people's ideas.

► Use your mental oasis to work through the problem. When you are relaxed it's a lot easier to come to a satisfactory conclusion.

► Accept the fact that your goals are your personal vision. Not everyone will see them.

▶ Consider the option of walking away. It takes two to fight. Why go through the wall if there is a possibility of going around it?

▶ Avoid questions that keep you blocked e.g. 'Why are they treating me this way? Why can't I make them understand?' More useful questions are 'How can I make this work for me? How can I communicate my message without alienating the other party or offending? How can I increase my ability to listen to the other side of the argument and not be dismissive?'

When situations don't go according to plan, there are some good coaching questions you can ask yourself to determine what you have learnt from the experience and how you can prevent it happening in the future. These include:

▶ How would I do it differently next time?

▶ What have I learned about myself from this experience?

▶ Can this situation be avoided in the future?

Use these questions to review past experiences. To be a really good coach there has to be a constant process of assessment and reassessment, otherwise you will continue to experience the same old blocks. The more painful the memory the more potential you have to learn an invaluable lesson. If you constantly view something from the same position, it's likely that you will keep seeing the same picture. To fine-tune your ability to communicate it's essential to move around. If you don't, you will still be approaching life from the same position.

▪ Positive Communicators

How you communicate gives a very strong message about the sort of person you are. There are individuals who can communicate a very strong message, but that message can be negative, e.g. a boss addressing his or her staff with the statement 'I'm definitely not going to be able to consider your request to pay a commission on sales.' There is nothing ambiguous about this communication: it couldn't be clearer, but the message it gives is negative, and indicates that the boss is not taking an open-minded approach. There is not much room for compromise here, is there? Obviously it's not only important how you communicate but also what is being communicated.

To keep things simple, I will describe four character traits that you will regularly encounter. Adopting any of the first three traits will keep you blocked. Let me tell you why:

1. The Opposer

The opposer constantly sees a reason to throw a spanner in the works. From the smallest decision to the biggest they think it's a bad idea. Even when the situation does not affect them they feel a need to give input.

- ► You are telling a work colleague that you plan to take a vacation to Bali. Despite the fact the colleague has never visited Bali their response is: 'I wouldn't go there if I was you. It's far too hot and the culture is completely different from ours.'

- ► Your company introduces a policy of flexi-hours, to which the opposer says: 'Why should I have to work flexi-hours just because some people can't get to work on time? What was wrong with the old system?'

- ► Having spent the last five years visiting the same family member for Christmas dinner you decide to invite the family to your home. Everyone accepts but the opposer says 'Well we didn't do that last year and we had a perfectly nice time, so why should we change this year?'

- ► You tell a friend about a goal you have, but their response is: 'I wouldn't do that if I were you.'

Opposers have strong character traits. They are opposed to change, and quick to present a problem with never a solution to follow. The opposer does not demonstrate qualities of leadership.

You may be curious as to why anyone would choose to join the opposition party. Perhaps the attraction lies in the element of safety. While constantly opposing, you never have to put yourself on the line. Forget your own agenda: you can always deflect attention from your own camp when you highlight the mess in other people's.

How to deal with the opposer

► Resist the temptation to defend yourself: the opposer is not open to seeing your point of view.

► Don't take their comments personally: their nature is to resist change.

► Use their negative comments to your own advantage as they can give you a different perspective on the situation.

► The world is full of opposers, so it's better to expect to come across them.

2. The Whinger

Or should I say the serial whinger? The funny thing about the whinger is they love to talk about other whingers. Ask them how they are feeling and they'll say, 'Oh, I'm OK, it's the rest of them.' So a typical conversation could run along these lines:

► 'Well I would have got my work in on time if so-and-so hadn't let me down.'

► 'I try to stay cheerful but my husband/wife is such an old misery they're always moaning.'

► 'I am sick to death putting myself out for the kids; they are such an ungrateful lot.'

► 'What's the point of having goals if everyone else is so negative about them?'

The common denominator is that it's always someone else's fault. The responsibility never lies with the whinger. Excuses are a way of life. If you find that your conversations are turning into one long moan, there's a good chance you're on your way to becoming a whinger.

How to deal with the whinger

► Take care not to get into competitive conversations, e.g. the whinger relays a moan to you and go one better with a moan of your own.

► If you are feeling despondent or negative about something, don't discuss it with the whinger. You'd feel a whole lot worse after an encounter with them.

► Keep your thought processes and conversation positive, and the whinger will be far less likely to seek out your company.

3. The fence-sitter

There are times when it is appropriate to sit on the fence while you're weighing up a decision. The trick is not to stay there too long or you will be blocked by apathy. At some point you have to make a decision unless you want to sit around and have decisions made for you. While it's not always prudent to rush a decision, if you find yourself continually coming up with 'I don't know where I'm going' or 'I don't know what to make of the situation', it's time to jump off.

When you have a firm sense of direction you do not need to spend a long time sitting on the fence. View the fence as a hurdle, and at times a temporary resting-place. But ultimately it has to be overcome.

How to deal with the fence-sitter:

Ask them some good coaching questions, such as:

► What is it you really want?

► What would make you feel better about this situation?

► What would be the best possible outcome for you, and how could you make it work for you?

► While you may find it frustrating that some individuals find it difficult to make a decision, it's worth recognising that everyone moves at a different pace.

4. The Ideas Person

The ideas person still encounters problems and blocks, but is committed to overcoming them. They like to set goals, find solutions to problems, find a positive message, communicate effectively and refuse to let excuses get in the way. Their ideas matter to them, and they don't lose hope when plans don't seem to be going their way. Ideas pave the way to your future success. For something to be a good idea it has first to be acknowledged by you. Does that sound like you?

▪ Conclusion

► Make sure you are communicating the right message.

► Relate positively to the word 'compromise'.

► If you want to communicate effectively, identify people who are good communicators and work on improving your existing skills.

► Communication is a two-way process that means providing space to listen and receive feedback.

► No one likes criticism: it can block communication. You are responsible for the nature and the content of all the information you present. Equally you can choose how you respond to incoming information.

► Using your journal, list the areas of communication you would like to work on, previous patterns you do not wish to repeat, and the future strategies you would like to take on.

PART 2

Seven Steps to Changing Your Life

Introduction

Part 1 of this book is an overview of the seven key steps of the life coaching programme. The focus was on equipping you with the relevant skills to determine your values in relation to your goals, getting you in the right frame of mind, overcoming any blocks you may experience, allocating the necessary time for making changes and learning how to communicate effectively.

In Part 2, each chapter deals with one of the seven steps in detail. The aim is to give you a step-by-step guide to working through your forms and getting the best possible results from your coaching programme. There may be times when you find it necessary to revert back to Part 1. If for example you are working through a particular form and feel blocked by negative thoughts, refer back to Chapter 3 (Developing a Positive Mental Attitude), or if the same old excuses keep coming up review Chapter 5 (No More Excuses).

In each of the following chapters there are practical exercises that will help to sharpen your focus on that particular area. So far you may have found it difficult to fill in some of your forms or you may have some forms that are incomplete, don't worry, Part 2 will provide you with the additional prompts you need.

A common occurrence with my clients is that they are only interested in being coached in what they see as their problem areas. You may hold a similar view and only refer to the chapters that seem relevant to you. But this is not a balanced approach. Just as everything may not be good in your life, all is certainly not bad. It would therefore not be prudent to only focus on the areas of your life that are problematic as you are likely to feel overloaded and inclined to overlook a healthy balance in other areas. Remember, if you want to achieve balance in your life, give equal attention to each of the seven steps.

Use the case histories in this section to practise your coaching skills. With each case history you read I would like you to use your journal to write down what techniques you would use to coach a particular client through their problem.

You don't have to take what I say as the conclusive result or only option available. After all, you have a valuable insight and may well see alternative options more suitable to your own situation. One of the best ways to become a truly effective coach is by extending your knowledge and experience to other people's problems. With a genuine desire to coach someone through a crisis you will find that your own level of awareness is greatly expanded. This means when it comes to dealing with your own life, you can benefit first hand from what you have learned. Make life coaching an interactive part of your life, share what you have learned with others. If you want to master the seven steps, you have to practise the skills you have learned, so keep practising on yourself and others. As I said earlier in this book 'Coach and be coached'.

CHAPTER EIGHT

Are You Fit for Life?

M Y CLIENTS vary from celebrities and politicians to housewives and business executives. Some give a lot of attention to their health and well-being; some don't. The great thing about coaching is that it's not one of those work-out routines that you can't even contemplate doing unless you're already super-fit because your coaching programme takes into account your individual needs. The emphasis in this chapter is to make you aware of what *your* needs are and how they can best be met. Coaching will push you beyond your normal boundaries by helping you to see beyond the limiting patterns that may be keeping you blocked.

I can certainly recall from my days in the beauty industry clients who would spend a small fortune on skincare products and keeping their bodies in prime condition. There were also those who were prompted to see me because they had let their bodies deteriorate or had encountered a major health problem. And yet, being fit goes beyond the superficial bodywork maintenance that you indulge yourself with at the health club. In our present cul-ture, more so than at any other time, there is a greater emphasis on a healthy mind, body and soul. Even activities such as t'ai chi, t'ai kwon do etc., which were once thought of as pastimes for hippies and sandal wearers, have found their way into the mainstream.

Mental stamina is phenomenally powerful. It's no wonder that your body struggles to keep up with it. Although your body is equally capable of high performance, the problem arises when the two are out of sync. You may start off with a healthy body, but when your energy levels sink, apathy soon sets in. An active mind can lead to hours of studious learning, but without the necessary exercise and nutrients your body will experience atrophy. The two are dependent on each other. To maximise one you have to service the other.

EXERCISE

Just to help you get things in perspective, spend a few minutes thinking about the following points. (You might want to use your journal to work this out.)

1. Have a look through your bathroom cabinet, dressing table, make-up bag and medicine cabinet.

2. Work out how much you spend on yourself in terms of grooming products and treatments, vitamin supplements, visits to the gym or beauty salon, exercise equipment and tapes, self-help books and relaxation techniques.

3. Now try and assess what your overall annual budget is.

4. Once you have done that, compare it to the annual budgets for some of the following: dry cleaning bills, car service and maintenance, house maintenance and insurance. In fact, you can include anything else on the list that requires regular maintenance and servicing.

5. Now compare your annual budget from point 3 with one of those in point 4 that you've just worked out. For example your annual budget for point 3 may have been £400 on grooming products and your annual dry cleaning budget in point 4 may have been £600.

Have you spotted the odd one out on the list of figures you've just worked out? All the items are replaceable – except for you. When you consider that the skin you are born with is the largest organ in the body and the only overcoat you get, it does seems strange to spend more on replaceable accessories. What you do with your disposable income is very much a case of personal preference. However, you have to be in a position to enjoy it.

Life makes many demands on your body and we've already established that problems go with the territory. Looking after your body puts you in the best position to go in prepared for the next challenge.

There is no doubt, though, that keeping the brain active will keep you mentally alert. Goals give you a sense of purpose, a reason to get out of bed in the morning. That's why you need to keep setting goals. Your mental and physical preparation is equally important. I've witnessed many people achieving goals without attending to their body in the process. No matter how many times we hear the saying 'You haven't got anything without your health', it often takes a crisis before the words really sink in. It did in my case, but it doesn't have to be the same for you.

▪ Setting Goals

It's time to get going with the goals in your health chart. By now you may have set a few: if not, now is a good time to start this. I'll give you some further examples of goals set by clients and show you how to prevent setting goals that put you in a negative frame of mind, are unsuitable to you or are limiting.

First, study the list of goals below:

► Lose weight

► Drink less alcohol

► Stop eating chocolate

► Give up junk food

Those all sound like worthwhile goals, don't they? The type that tend to appear on many a New Year's resolution. And yet, surveys have shown that within forty-eight hours of setting resolutions, most people have given into temptation and done at least one if not several of the things on their list. So what went wrong? Is it so difficult to stick to goals? Thankfully, no. The problem lies in dealing with some pretty stiff opposition, i.e. your own willpower. The focus of most of the above goals means depriving yourself of something that you probably enjoy. In the case of the goal 'lose weight', you may be reinforcing a very negative body image. So let's look at the alternatives and see why they are so much more effective.

If you group together the goals that involve giving something up – chocolate, junk food and alcohol – you are keeping the focus of your brain on those things. So if you constantly keep reminding yourself not to eat chocolate, there's a good chance you will trigger an almighty craving for it. After all, you will be thinking about it more than usual. Then, when you do give in to temptation you'll feel bad about your lack of willpower. But the funny thing is that each time you are doing battle with yourself and unwittingly setting yourself up for failure. If anything, your willpower is winning the day because it wants the chocolate. You have planted a really strong message in both the conscious and subconscious mind and that message is – I want chocolate, now!

Goals are much easier to achieve when there is a reward attached to them. Obviously a healthy body is a great reward, but you may have lost sight of that. Instead, the brain is concerning itself with a sense of loss because you are telling yourself what you can't have. Shifting your focus and rewording your goals can have an amazing impact. The goals will change as follows:

ORIGINAL GOALS	**GOALS WITH A POSITIVE FOCUS**
Lose weight	Exercise and get in shape
Drink less alcohol	Drink eight glasses of water a day
Stop eating chocolate	Buy healthy foods/eat a healthy diet
Give up junk food	Learn more about healthy foods

Now you can watch these goals progress.

You have your goal in place, and it's a positive goal, e.g. to eat a healthy diet. Underneath the section entitled Immediate Challenges/Blocks/Problems you can list any problems that are getting in the way of your goal, for example you may be eating too much junk food or not getting the necessary nutrients in your diet. From identifying the problem you can move on to finding a solution. You have lots of options here and I'm going to give you a few more.

First you can offer solutions that address your shopping list. If you are eating a poor diet, one glance at your cupboards and fridge may show that you have got into the habit of buying convenience foods. But on the subject of convenience foods, take a look at the carton or outer sleeve of a quick fix meal. I bet it looks really good. The food industry has really cracked that formula; they know just how to appeal to your taste buds.

But now that you're in solution mode, it's time to outsmart them and increase or improve some of your development skills. What your goal needs is a game plan. It's not enough to stick down 'a healthy diet'. Goals require your participation. Keeping your focus on achieving a healthy diet is also a much healthier mind-set to be in. The emphasis is on the good, not the bad.

Here's the plan:

1. Start with your shopping. You will be less inclined to buy convenience foods if you shop in a large supermarket where there is a greater selection. Trying to food-shop as you go doesn't work, especially if you shop when you are hungry. You'll be much more likely to fill a basket with stodgy convenience foods.

2. Invest in some good cookery books. If you're in the habit of buying convenience foods it can be difficult to put a meal together from scratch. Most supermarkets have a cookery book section. Spend some time reading cooking instructions. Serving suggestions will give you ideas for meals.

3. Time doesn't have to be an issue. When you plan ahead and equip yourself with information about food, preparing healthy food becomes less time-consuming.

4. Make your shopping trolley look exciting by filling it with colourful and interesting-looking food. I'm sure, like me, you are inclined to look at what other people have bought when you queue at the checkout. We've all seen the trolleys full of biscuits, crisps, fizzy drinks, frozen foods, cakes and pastries. And observed the people buying them. They often present a good case for the maxim 'You are what you eat'. Try and add at least one new food item to your shopping every week.

5. Make your fridge look interesting. Give some thought to how you can display your food to make it look inviting.

One of my clients drew smiling faces on her eggs. It may sound silly, but previously she had regularly thrown out cartons of eggs because she always overlooked them.

6. Work on your development skills. Increase your knowledge about food and cooking. You don't have to become a top chef, but if you really want to ditch the convenience foods you have to know how to flavour food and make it taste good. Many convenience foods are so highly salted and sugared that your own food may taste bland until you re-educate your taste buds and learn how to prepare tasty alternatives.

I often recommend to clients that they visit a nutritionist. Few people think to do this. But who better to advise you on a healthy eating plan? A nutritionist can give you a personal assessment based on your health, age, weight, genetic predisposition and personal requirements. Their advice can prove invaluable and also stop you from purchasing unsuitable or unnecessary supplements. There are also some very good books available on nutrition (see Further Reading).

As for goals that are based on losing weight, again I would encourage you to keep your focus on a healthy diet. You may find that having a goal to get in shape and improve fitness levels is far less likely to reinforce a negative body image. To do that, you might consider enrolling at a gym or fitness class, as well as increasing development skills and congratulating yourself on your achievements. When weight is the issue many individuals find it hard to stay motivated. If you are setting this goal, give some thought to how you want to word it and the message you are giving yourself. Focus on where you are going, not where you are coming from.

Take a look at Mary's form and think about how you would coach her:

- **Goals:** lose weight, take up exercise when I have lost weight.
- **Problems/challenges/blocks:** I feel so depressed about my weight and lack of will-power. The more 'down' I feel, the more I eat. My husband is a very intolerant and impatient man and

when he picks on me I eat more. I have a wardrobe full of clothes that don't fit, I get breathless because of my weight and my joints ache.

Mary left the Personal strengths, Development skills and Achievements sections blank.

After some discussion, Mary's form changed to:

- **Goals:** Eat a healthier diet; look after my body; pamper myself; adopt a healthier lifestyle; get more fresh air and exercise.
- **Problems/challenges/blocks:** I need to work on my motivation and self-esteem.

Mary was now working on achieving positive goals and identifying her problem in a way that didn't make her feel like a failure before she started.

With the focus on healthy eating it was now possible to set Mary a few challenges. First she visited a nutritionist, whom she found inspirational. She suffered from asthma and was surprised to learn that certain food groups might be aggravating her breathlessness. Gaining additional knowledge about food groups encouraged Mary to be selective about what she bought.

Once Mary got the motivation she needed, there was no stopping her, and over the next few months, her achievements included joining a health club, taking up regular exercise, buying a new wardrobe of flattering clothes, having a weekly massage and monthly facials, attending the occasional yoga class and reaching her target weight! And Mary achieved her goals without undergoing a major personality transplant.

You can do this too. It's just a case of incorporating changes that will move you forward. Often, breaking a problem down allows you to find a workable solution. When you list each new achievement your confidence will grow along with your motivation. Because thoughts govern your actions, your goal has to be positive to allow you to think about it in a positive way and trigger the necessary motivation to achieve it. This can simply involve rewording your goal, or problem. To keep your motivation flowing you have to remind yourself of the progress you are making, so use your file and journal. If you experience a setback you can quickly get back on track by reminding yourself how far you have come. If you are struggling to list achievements and development skills, review your goals again. Make sure they are not worded in such a way as to keep you blocked.

In the case study above, I've deliberately picked an extreme example of an individual who was clearly finding it very difficult to get the motivation she needed. It would be unfair to think that Mary didn't want to change her situation, as I truly believe she did, but sometimes we create such a block for ourselves that self-esteem takes a real battering in the process. I may not be a dietician, but as a personal coach I do know something about learning how to set goals that move you forward rather than using ones that merely identify the problem and keep you stuck. Just as adopting a healthy lifestyle and diet can involve a process of re-education, so does goal-setting. You may have set goals for yourself in the past, only to feel disappointed when they are not realised. But the best way to climb any mountain is to take a step at a time.

There are many things you can incorporate into your health chart by making a few minor adjustments. You can walk more, take the stairs instead of the lift, play some music and dance around the sitting room, practise breathing techniques, and do some gentle stretches. I'm not suggesting that everyone sign up for a high-impact aerobic class or strenuous circuit training. Even if you manage to escape injury, you'll pay the price the following day with muscle fatigue. So be sensible: it might be a good idea to have a medical check-up before you set out to improve your fitness level. At any rate, gather information and talk to the experts. Most good fitness centres now provide personal trainers who can devise the right routine for you. Can you imagine how much better it would be to have something tailor-made to your needs rather than expecting your body to conform to an unsuitable exercise programme?

Summary

1. Make your goal a positive one that reflects what you want to bring into your life, not what you want to eliminate. A good working example is as follows:

Goal	Get fit
Problem	Time management
Personal strength	Reasonably healthy with no major physical problems
Development skill	Do one hour of exercise a week
Achievement	Enrolled in aerobics class

2. Include as many personal strengths, development skills and achievements as possible. Look for ones that relate to the goals you have set, so that you are encouraged.

3. Incorporate your health plan into as many areas of your life as possible. Your health plan shouldn't just revolve around a weekly trip to the gym.

4. If necessary, break your goal down into smaller, more manageable steps. That way you can more quickly make progress and note your achievements.

5. Gather information so as not to miss opportunities that are easily overlooked.

Now that you're under way you are ready for a few challenges. You'll need your file and journal for the next exercise.

EXERCISE

Make a list in your journal of all the things you can do to improve your health chart. The more imaginative you are the better. Run through your average day listing all the changes you could make. I'll help you to get in the mood with a few suggestions: get up earlier and practise breathing techniques; buy a juicer and kick off the day with a high energy drink; walk to work; cut out the health section from magazines; buy some aromatherapy oils for your bath; drink more water; get some leaflets from the local health club. If you are sitting down for most of the day at work, why not find out about some good ergonomic chairs?

Your health chart can have a low score when you limit the things to include in it. There are many things that contribute to your health and well-being, so be sure you aren't overlooking them. If you include visits to the gym and don't follow through with them, don't overlook other achievements. If necessary, review a goal again, e.g. at the end of a stressful day you might not feel like going to the gym. A less vigorous exercise may be more attractive and just as beneficial. It's easy to assume that the goals we set must be good for us because they aren't much fun!

You should be aiming to contribute to your health on a daily basis. By exploring every avenue you will soon see how easy it is to begin with small changes and work up to bigger ones. You will also be less inclined to swing from one extreme to another. By gradually making changes to your routine it's much easier to make them an integral part of your life. All good work-outs start with a warm-up.

And The Goal Got Bigger

When you make progress with any goal your motivational bank account is rewarded. This can and often does inspire you to achieve even more. One of the most inspiring stories I have ever come across was that of Daphne Belt.

At the age of fifty, Daphne was overweight and so unfit that she wheezed when she walked up a hill. Although Daphne had never previously been fit or sporty she set herself a modest enough goal to exercise her way to good health and slimness. But as the new Daphne began emerging, she began to think big. Bit by bit – and the transformation was nothing short of remarkable – she became a world-class athlete. At the age of fifty-eight, Daphne was Britain's oldest long-distance female triathlete (which involves swimming 2.4 miles, cycling 112 miles and running a full 26-mile marathon) with sixteen medals under her belt.

Can you imagine the effort that went into such an achievement? Setting a goal to become a triathlete would probably have been unthinkable when Daphne first started out. But it just goes to show you what you are capable of when you put your mind to it. You can change your goals as you go along. When your self-esteem is low, a much better approach is to find ways of overcoming the minor hurdles and work your way up to the bigger ones. If a previous goal has always seemed out of reach, you may be inadvertently repeating old patterns that result in failure. So start off with some minor changes and watch your confidence grow.

▪ Action Plans

Once you have your goals in place there has to be a plan of action. Lots of people express a desire to do something without giving any thought as to how. You may have a goal to visit the gym two evenings a week and then list in the problem section 'I'm often required to work late and at short notice'. If you leave the situation there your goal won't materialise. The work situation may be beyond your control, especially if you have the type of job where working overtime is very much part of the culture.

Setting health goals that are easily interfered with suggests you are not giving enough priority to this area. You can't tag your health goal on at the end of a day that you know is subject to change. The goal becomes secondary, no more than an after-thought that you will fit in if and when time allows. It's not so much a case of poor time management as inappropriate time management. Study your week carefully: perhaps a visit to the gym would be better first thing in the morning or at weekends. I'm often surprised by how few people see their health plan fitting into a weekend. For some reason the working week is seen as the time to be busy and cram everything in. Possibly the biggest risk with this is that your health plan is not truly seen as a treat, a benefit, a means to relax. Your health should not be exclusive to particular days. Allocate times you know are unlikely to be subject to change.

To help you with your action plan let's look at a few goals and watch them progress.

Goals
1. Exercise regularly and get in shape
2. Eat a healthier diet

With goal 1 it would immediately help to define what is meant by 'regular exercise', as it could be 'daily' to one person and 'weekly' to another. Also, be clear about what you mean by 'get in shape'. List the things you want to improve which can include: cardiovascular fitness, strength, stamina, suppleness, muscle tone and definition. Think about the desired outcome of your programme and give some thought to the type of exercise that you wish to do. By gathering information you'll have more options and know if a particular exercise will produce the desired results. Just as your health shouldn't exclude any day, it doesn't have to exclude any area. Incorporate it into as many areas as possible from starting the day with breathing techniques, to doing abdominal exercises if you're sitting at work all day, or learning some eye exercises if you work on a computer screen.

Unless you are already very fit don't try setting a punishing schedule. Make small changes to begin with by setting smaller goals on a daily basis. Be careful about the time you set aside – are you being realistic? It may be far better to attend one regular class than running around trying to juggle several.

Set some deadlines. If your health plan is open-ended you may never get round to doing it, or you'll get distracted by other things. Referring to your journal and file on a regular basis will keep you focused on your goals. At the end of the week you can assess your progress and add to your personal strengths and achievements.

As an exercise, work out an action plan for goal 2 (Eat a healthier diet). Then you can get to work on your own goals.

▪ Health form

The information above should enable you to complete your own form. Go through what you have written making any revisions you feel are necessary. Here are a few additional ideas to show you the sort of thing you should include.

Goals
- Eat a healthy diet
- Visit a nutritionist
- Have a weekly massage
- Practise relaxation techniques, such as breathing exercises
- Drink more water
- Take regular exercise
- Improve my muscle tone and flexibility

Personal strengths

- I am reasonably healthy and have no major health problems
- I enjoy exercising
- I am committed to achieving a healthier body
- I am not overweight
- I value the importance of a healthy body
- I appreciate how much better my body performs when I take care of it

Immediate challenges/blocks/problems

- I find it difficult to get motivated
- I have a tendency to overload my schedule and not allocate enough time for exercise
- When I feel stressed I eat/drink/smoke too much

Development skills

- Work on my motivation on a daily basis and use affirmations to reinforce my self-esteem
- Learn more about food and nutrition
- Learn to take time out for myself
- Learn to recognise the signals when my body feels stressed
- Include a new skill in my fitness programme i.e. yoga, meditation, roller skating, Latin dancing

Achievements

- I have joined a health club
- I got the all clear from my annual medical
- I rarely get colds or other illnesses
- My fitness level is above average for my age
- I completed a five-mile charity run
- I have stuck to a low-fat diet for the last year
- I have given up smoking
- I cycle to work every day

Remember to set goals that will put you in a positive frame of mind. Use affirmations to reinforce your personal strengths and achievements. Look at your problems as challenges to be worked through and overcome and remember to make out an action plan for dealing with these. Continually gather information for your folder to inspire you with ideas and new skills to develop and add to your achievement list every time you make progress in this area.

▪ Conclusion

► List as many things as possible that can be included in your health programme.

► Start with smaller goals and work your way up to bigger ones.

► Be realistic about how you allocate time. Set aside a time that is unlikely to be subject to change.

► Impose some deadlines for achieving your goal.

► Have a plan of action.

CHAPTER NINE

Spiritual and Religious Life

THE SPIRITUAL/RELIGIOUS form is optional to clients, although as I mentioned earlier you may find yourself coming back to it even if you initially chose to leave it out. The reasons vary. Problems may cause you to want answers or seek some divine purpose and explanation. Perhaps, as you prioritise your value system, you may question what influenced your choice. When you make mission statements it can provoke major questions such as 'What is the purpose of my life?' or 'Why am I here?'

I would encourage you to visit this area and make some contribution to the form. Experience has taught me that to avoid it indicates a block, as self-exploration operates at a very deep level. There is never any pressure on clients to complete this section, nor is there any on you. If your initial reaction is to leave this form out the only question I would leave you with is 'Why?' If you are clear about your answer then you may feel ready to move on to the next chapter. On the other hand if you have some questions of your own this chapter may throw some light on them. You will also have the chance to review your mission statements again and outline your value system.

The form for this section is no different from any of the other forms. You may be wondering if it can be tackled using the same approach as the other areas in your life chart. The answer is 'Yes it can', which may prompt you to ask 'How can that be? After all there are no definitive solutions or answers in this section.' I agree, but the same could be said for the rest of the seven steps. There is no right or wrong solution or answer for everyone. What makes it right is when it's right for you. That's why it's so important to find your own solutions and understand what influences your choices. The same rules apply.

▪ Identifying Goals

Let's begin by looking at some goals. Remember that this is not the place to identify problems, or – as is often the case with this form – pose open-ended questions such as 'What is my destiny?' or 'How can I find a way to stop my family imposing religion on me?' Goals are about what you want to bring into your life and are part of your own personal quest. Equally, be careful about setting goals for other people, like 'I want my children to marry someone of the same religion.' Religious beliefs are clearly close to some people's hearts and while you are at liberty to impose the requirements of a religious doctrine, it can't be viewed as a goal for the purposes of coaching.

This list may help you to identify a few of your own goals. If you are still finding it difficult to be clear about your goals, use your journal to write out the thoughts that come to mind. At this stage you may find it easier to write out questions or random statements which can include: 'I don't know if I have any particular belief'; 'I can't see the significance of this area'; 'Why do I need to have any spiritual/religious conviction?'; 'What exactly am I trying to get in touch with?' and 'I sometimes feel there is something missing – but I'm not sure what.' Write down whatever thought comes to mind rather than trying to make sense of them in your head or putting up an intellectual argument. Thoughts can defy all logic so why not try and expand on your questions before searching for conclusive answers? Asking questions can put you in touch with your goals, but only if you ask the right ones, for example 'How can I get in touch with my faith?' or 'How can I become more spiritually enlightened?' will move you forward, whereas 'Why am I not in touch with my faith?' or 'Why am I not more spiritually enlightened?' will keep you blocked. The 'why' questions are rarely useful especially about a subject matter based on a belief system that may require no evidence to back it up.

While there are no definitive answers on this subject, there is no shortage of books that attempt to unravel the many mysteries of life. As with all your other goals, information will help to move you forward and you may feel yourself drawn to read a particular book or recall one that made a strong impression on you. When something has made an impact, use your journal to identify what it was that struck you. Perhaps it calls for further exploration on your part. Information has a way of presenting itself when you request it. Sometimes a mental request is enough. The explanation for this is not necessarily mysterious, since you have put your brain on alert mode. Information that may have previously escaped your attention is no longer overlooked. However if you chose to overlook this area completely you may be pursuing answers from an inappropriate section.

I chose to place the chapter on values and goals deliberately early in this book, because so many individuals have achieved a goal only to find it didn't have the desired result. Perhaps it would be more accurate to say it didn't make them feel how they thought it would. Without putting aside some time for self-exploration it's very difficult to be in touch with what's really important to you. Some people learn this the hard way when they experience a loss, or put all their energies into pursuing goals that are not rewarding, or push themselves to the brink of a physical and mental break-down. No matter how fast you run, you can never run away from yourself.

Regardless of how much acclaim you receive for achieving a particular goal, nothing replaces personal satisfaction. I'm sure we have all met people who seem to have so much on the surface, but when you dig a little deeper they act as if they have nothing. Is it simply that some people are never satisfied? But what you perceive as being valuable may hold no value to another person. Despite the fact that they may have pursued material possessions, they may never have questioned why they wanted them. Assumptions are made along the way. The definition of success may be a learned one or an imposed one. From an early age you may have been under pressure to achieve in education, sport, music and so on. This is hardly surprising since we live in a society that is competitive in terms of who has the brightest baby, the most attractive partner, the most talented students, the best paid job, the biggest house and so on.

Throughout your life you can find yourself contending with both your own expectations and those of others. I can't help but cringe every time I hear the words 'What a waste of a good education', especially when they refer to someone who has chosen a career that makes them happy. Education is never wasted. Life is a huge learning curve from beginning to end. But isn't it surprising that we are rarely given the opportunity to learn about ourselves? Why is this seen by so many as such a selfish pursuit? I wanted to introduce these questions into this section because I am sure that many of you have a great desire to explore the self. Anyone can achieve goals: believe me, it's not difficult. But will they bring you what you want? And how are you supposed to get what you want if you don't actually know?

So, as always, let's be specific and set goals that relate to you, that are clearly defined and, above all, that you believe are achievable. Study the list below.

1. Stay true to my religion.

2. Meditate on a daily basis.

3. Increase my knowledge and understanding of other spiritual teachings.

4. Treat others as I wish to be treated.

5. Get in touch with my higher self.

6. Go to church (or wherever) every Sunday (or whenever).

7. Become involved in charity work.

With every goal you set, take the time to question what difference it will make to your life if you achieve it. Ask yourself if you are doing it for yourself or to impress/please others. Do you feel you have something to prove and, if so, what? Have you really explored the reasons behind why you want this goal? Does this goal reflect your value system and spiritual/religious path?

You see, there is some point in achieving something for the sake of achievement alone. It will mean little to you, if anything. True success can only be defined on a personal level, which involves thinking about what would make you happy rather than what would gain attention or impress others. The achievement stage is usually the most enjoyable part of the whole process. Even when you really want to achieve a goal, you can feel a sense of anti-climax at the point when it is realised. Not because the goal is not a worthy one for you, but because you feel somewhat despondent without something to work for and put your energy into. It's fun working on your own projects, and as one nears completion, it's time to give some thought to the next one. Otherwise you stand still. Without something to work on you can't see what progress you have made, and you will quickly feel like you are slipping back rather than moving forward. You may see each goal as a very separate project, but that is a tricky plan to work with. However much you try to keep the areas of your life separate you can't because you are the one element common to every level. And into them you take your values, beliefs, code of conduct, opinions and every other component that makes you the individual you are.

▪ Drawing up a Mission Statement

By having an overall game plan you'll soon see how various goals do or don't fit into your life. Conflicting goals are far less obvious without an encompassing mission statement. In the following list, I'd like you to give some thought to the type of mission statement that you feel reflects your life and whether they have any spiritual/religious relevance. Here are some examples:

► My mission in life is to follow a path of spiritual growth.

► My mission in life is to make a contribution to humanity and the environment.

► My mission in life is to stay true to my religious teachings.

► My mission in life is to be open minded and non-judgemental.

► My mission in life is to make as much money as possible.

► My mission in life is to be famous and go down in history.

► My mission in life is to be happy and have as much fun as possible.

► My mission in life is to always be there for my family and loved ones.

Mission statements do vary, without a doubt. The important thing is that you are in touch with your overall purpose in life. You also need to see how your values fit in to that. If your mission is to make as much money as possible and values have no significance to you, you might be inclined to do something illegal, like insider trading. Of course there are consequences that shouldn't be overlooked. While the peccadillo you have committed may not be worthy of a prison sentence, behaving in a way that you believe is wrong can lead to your finding a way to punish yourself. This starts to become obvious when you set conflicting goals. No matter how much you try to keep your attention on the final goal, you still have to contend with the bit in the middle. You've already seen this in some of the case histories, such as that of Melanie who was emotionally caught up in an affair with a married man, but paid the price of a guilty conscience. And John who opted for the high salary and long working hours, which didn't compensate for the loss of family time.

Balance, as I have often said, is the key to your coaching programme. With this in mind you can see why you need to give attention to every one of the seven steps and not view them separately.

On the subject of money, clients are often curious to know if they can pursue commercial goals and still incorporate their personal spiritual beliefs. Well, everything is open to interpretation – which means your interpretation, not mine. There is a quote in the Bible that says 'It is harder for a camel to go through the eye of a needle than for a rich man to enter the gates of Heaven'. If you hold that particular belief then you could still possibly pursue a commercial goal for a particular reason, but be swayed to sabotage it along the way or give away all the proceeds. Whatever belief you hold will influence the decisions you make and the final outcome of the situation. You need to be aware of your own personal participation in the event and what the goal really means to you. I don't have a scale of good or bad goals, and you're not working to some hidden agenda. The objective you have set yourself is that you are working towards something you want to achieve in your life, not something you want to eliminate.

▪ Finding out what you want

The important thing is to become familiar with identifying what it is you want. It seems a practice long since forgotten, and you may be afraid to ask for what you want, but if someone is going to burst the bubble, perhaps you think you should be the one to do it. But be careful of self-imposed restrictions. The biggest block you contend with is often yourself. You can find lots of excuses and you can even hide behind your own belief system. All I ask you to do is be aware of what is holding you back. If you feel that a particular belief system was engrained in you as a child, you have the platform as an adult to deal with it. You can question what your own beliefs are and find a way to incorporate them into your life. You now have the opportunity to set your own goals and be the active player, not the spectator on the sidelines. You have the opportunity to ask the questions and provide the answers. The bigger the challenge, the bigger the reward.

So here is a challenge. Take out your journal and start writing. Let it flow, because what I want you to do is write about your own personal beliefs, which can range from 'I do/don't believe in God' and 'I do/don't believe in life after death' to 'I do/don't believe it's wrong to have sex before marriage', 'I do/don't believe you should only have children within the sanctuary of marriage' to 'I do/don't believe divorce is wrong' and 'I do/don't disapprove of abortion'. Do not only write about them but ask yourself the following questions: Where did they come from? Why do I believe them? How do they affect my life? Would I want to change them? If so, how? And what's stopping me? You have free scope and total freedom of expression.

The more you find out about yourself, the more in touch you will be with your goals. Your goals will start to have relevance to your life and be appropriate. It's an ongoing process and it is subject to change. So give yourself permission to make the necessary changes. Stop waiting for the jury to make judgement on you. Ultimately your own beliefs predict the final verdict.

The problem Anna presented me with at our first consultation was that she needed to find 'a way to contribute'. The problem for me was to find out exactly what she meant by 'contribute' and what areas of her life she saw this fitting into. I hoped that, by filling in her forms, she would provide me with the answer. Initially, though, Anna chose not to fill in her Spiritual/religious form.

As we worked through each of Anna's forms there appeared plenty of evidence of ways in which she did contribute. The relationship with her husband and children sounded healthy and fulfilling, her health was good, finances posed no problem, she was excited about a forthcoming Open University course, gave up a lot of her time willingly to charity work and yet we kept coming back to the area of contribution.

It was not obvious to Anna what the block was and in fact it was not obvious to me either. If anything, and probably like many people who knew Anna, I couldn't help but admire and praise her for her selflessness.

How could I help my client? Anna puzzled me. I decided to consult my mental oasis. I was concerned that I was missing something. We had reviewed all the areas of Anna's chart. Except one – the Spiritual/religious form. At our next session I asked Anna how she felt about filling it in as we had explored every other area of her chart and she was still searching for a way in which to contribute. 'OK,' she said, 'maybe it *is* time I took a look at that area.'

Anna faxed me the form a few days later with a covering letter. I have set out her letter here and I hope this will help you to understand why I am so keen to request that you don't overlook this area.

Dear Eileen,

I had never thought very seriously about religion, but two years ago when I was travelling with my husband we visited a Buddhist retreat on our way back from Malaysia. At the time I said to him that I would dearly love to return alone and spend some time there. My husband was all for it and positively encouraged me.

When we got home I felt that it would be unfair to leave my family and go in pursuit of I'm not quite sure what, so I left it.

Ever since my trip my curiosity for Eastern beliefs has turned into what I can only describe as a passion. I have read numerous books on the subject and find myself glued to the subject when it's on TV. As you know, I love history and perhaps that's why I treated my interest as that of a historian rather than a possible participant in the process.

Whenever I read a book I could always close it and somehow close that chapter in relation to my own life, but as you always say, the theory alone is not enough. I'm beginning to see where my contribution gulf is coming from. Somewhere deep inside me there is a space that needs filling. The contribution I seek is a personal one. 'Food for the soul' was the touching expression my husband used.

I think this must be the first time in my life I have ever taken the time to explore myself on this level. My eldest son thinks it's hysterical that mum is going off to find herself. He's taken to going around the house chanting 'Mum, Mum, Mum'. But all credit to them, they've all been really supportive.

Right now I'm feeling a mixture of giddy excitement, blind panic and I don't know what else. Needless to say I can't wait till our next session.

Sincerest thanks

Anna.

Anna's Form

Goals

- Go on a Buddhist retreat (I've booked to go next month for two weeks)
- Acknowledge the significance of many of the events in my life
- Contribute to my own spiritual growth

Immediate problems/challenges/blocks

- Always helping others has been my way of avoiding looking at myself
- I'm afraid to stop being the carer as it might be a bit of a shock to see how well my family gets on without me for a few weeks

Personal strengths

- When I make a commitment I stick to it
- My charity work

Development skills
- Take up meditation
- Learn more about other religions and beliefs
- Ask for help when I need it

Achievements
- I've got this far and there's no looking back

Coaching had encouraged Anna to explore an area that she had previously avoided. She was experiencing a huge contribution gulf but had been unable to pinpoint where it was coming from. Without the support of a coach, Anna may have continued to ignore or overlook this area, but the principle of coaching is to leave no stone unturned until a solution is found to a problem. The coach can bring a fresh pair of eyes to a situation, and may redirect you to look at something you had previously overlooked.

Every case history which has been included in this book makes an equal contribution. They all have their special point of relevance to each of us, but I hope you will allow me some personal input to say that when I read Anna's letter and form I was deeply moved. When a client follows through on a journey of personal exploration there are no words to express what takes place in that process. Only you can discover that for yourself. Maybe that's why I believe that the best coach is within you.

▪ Spiritual/Religious form

Now you have read this chapter, I hope that you have a better idea of how to complete this form, setting goals appropriate to your values and developing your personal awareness. Here are a few suggestions to help you on your way.

Goals
- Incorporate my spiritual beliefs into my life on a daily basis
- Become involved in a charitable organisation
- Go on a religious retreat
- Be more tolerant towards others

- Say my prayers every day
- Maintain my faith even when the going gets tough
- Meditate every day
- Be more loving and forgiving

Personal strengths
- My faith is a great comfort to me
- I have a strong conviction towards my beliefs
- I'm determined to make a bigger contribution
- I believe that God will direct me onto the right path
- I am open to making changes

Immediate challenges/blocks/problems
- I often feel judgemental and angry towards others
- When I experience major problems I feel like God has abandoned me
- I want to pursue a spiritual path, but feel afraid of the changes this could involve in my life
- It upsets me when other people ridicule my beliefs

Development skills
- Learn to love and accept myself
- Learn about other religions and spiritual teachings
- Trust what's in my heart and have the courage of my convictions
- Ask for guidance and support when I need it
- Be more open to new ideas
- Stop worrying about how other people judge me
- See good in others and not just the people who are nice to me
- Learn to give unconditionally without expecting to receive

Achievements
- I am aware of my shortfalls and am prepared to overcome them
- I am less self critical than I used to be
- I have discarded many of my old and limiting beliefs
- I have experienced the joy of love
- I have not abandoned my faith
- I have increased my capacity to love
- My life feels blessed

▪ Conclusion

► Make a contribution to this section.

► If you are unclear about your goals, keep asking prompting questions.

► Review your values.

► Make some mission statements that are reflective to your life in general.

► Make sure your goals are relevant to your personal mission statements and values.

► Practise some freedom of expression! Write down what you want and why you want it.

► If something is getting in the way of your goals, write it down and work on how you will deal with it. If you can find the problem the solution is waiting in line.

► Keep an open mind. The minute you think you have got a solution, be prepared to address the possibility that you've overlooked something.

CHAPTER TEN

Work and Career

I N THIS CHAPTER, we will be discussing what work you do and why you do it. For the majority of us, the working day takes up a major part of our lives, so it's important to get the most from your job. Because the workplace is never problem-free, knowing how to deal with stress is an essential skill and one that you need to master. If you are still looking for the right job, there are also techniques for creating the job you really want.

When it comes to the work you do, how clear are you about why you do it? There are usually many factors involved when it comes to making choices about work and career. It could be choice, necessity, or a combination of the two. Getting caught up in the daily routine may have caused you to overlook your reasons, but it's worth asking yourself why you made a particular career choice. One thing you can say for sure is that there will have been a whole sequence of events that led to your current employment status.

Job insecurity has become the 1990s work mantra, as if it were something new that had never previously posed a threat. In reality, job insecurity has always existed, and as technology advances it affects different sectors of the workplace. Technology has made some of the old skills redundant and created gaps for new ones. An abundance of statistics predict the way forward, some of which are confusing at best and contradictory at worst. Having said that, it's prudent to arm yourself with information. Why? Because then you can see that change is the norm rather than stability.

▪ Getting the Most from Your Job

When it comes to making a career choice you are in a far better position to do it if you equip yourself with more information. The culture of a company can make a huge impact on your working life. So it's worth knowing if they are family-friendly, offer term-time contracts, childcare, job sharing, ongoing training, stress management and so on. A company may have given little thought to how you can balance your life. You, on the other hand, need to give such matters a great deal of thought.

Whatever your status – married, single, divorced, in a relation-ship, or have children to support – you will have requirements for your well-being in the workplace which go beyond financial secu-rity and job satisfaction. There is no guarantee that your situation will remain the same and personal flexibility is as crucial as com-pany flexibility. Technology has without a doubt upped the pace of the changes taking place and you need to be aware of the movement going on around you in order to deal with the impli-cations. The more information you have, the more of an informed choice you can make. Life is not stationary anywhere within a company so it's no good closing your eyes and hoping for the best. The individuals who feel they have no control or choice are the ones who experience the greatest stress. They are swept along in the tide of change with no idea of what direction they are going in.

Because the changes are ongoing, so are the choices you will have to make. There may be a greater comfort factor in thinking you can make a choice, then wrap that area up and move on to another. But the chances are you will have to keep the file open at all times. Your Work and career form has to be reviewed regularly.

▪ The Stress Factor

How you view stress depends on how it affects you. Is it good for you, bad for you, all in the mind, given too much emphasis, or not enough? There probably isn't one conclusive answer that will suit everyone, as it will affect everyone differently. Looking out for some of the common signs, though, can give you some indication if you have cause for concern. Here are a few:

► Constant conflict at work

► Inability to concentrate and focus

► Feeling overwhelmed on a regular basis

► Mood swings and irrational behaviour

► Trouble sleeping or excessive sleeping

► Finding it difficult to switch off from work

► Niggling health problems ranging from stomach upsets to skin rashes and fatigue

► Substance abuse – alcohol, drugs

► An unmanageable workload

► You lose your sense of humour

If you are experiencing one or more of any of the above problems, use your journal to list them. Try to identify what the major ones are. Once you have done that, it will be easier to see if some problems are symptomatic of other ones. Here's an example: the major problem may be that you have an unmanageable work load and that, as a result, you constantly struggle to meet deadlines and regularly have confrontations with your boss. At times like this, confrontation can be the major stress trigger and the problem of an unrealistic workload may be overlooked, so try and get to the root cause of the problem. It will help you to see where the solution is required.

You can reduce the effects of stress when you find ways to control what is going on around you. There's no point pretending that you have control in certain areas when you know that's not the case. One of the things you can always control is your perception of what's going on. You can look at what upsets you, why you feel the way you do, and what you could do to feel differently. For example, are you slipping into a mind-set that is keeping you blocked? On a practical level you can make sure you are taking care of yourself – and bear in mind that vegging out in front of the television is not necessarily the best way to unwind after a stressful day. You'll benefit more from having interests outside work that allow you to switch off, such as regular exercise, eating a healthy diet, using breathing or relaxation techniques, talking your problems over with someone or writing them down. They'll look a whole lot less threatening on paper and, as you know, that can make it easier to find solutions. Also, have a look around the bookshops: there are some very good books on stress management.

And just in case you have underestimated how stress affects you in the workplace, here are a few statistics that you might find interesting.

Forty per cent of all absenteeism through sickness is attributed to stress-related psychological illness. The cost to the British economy alone is estimated at between £5–6 billion per year. The Department of Health calculates that, at any one time, 20 per cent of the workforce is having personal problems and that 30 per cent of the adult population suffer from depression and anxiety at some stage of their working life.

There are some steps being taken to improve the situation. The recent *Walker vs Northumberland County Council* case set a legal precedent by being the first case in which an employee established a link between stress at work and an emotional illness. As with most legal cases the grounds for pursuing such a claim are not that straightforward. In *Walker* the employee had suffered one nervous breakdown and a second one six months later as a result of his continued workload. The court's ruling was based on the evidence that the second breakdown should have been foreseen by the company, although there was no suggestion that the first one could. The case was successful because it presented the four major criteria for a personal injury claim: breach of the employer's duty of care; injury; causation; and foreseeability. The last two can be difficult to prove in practice. But this has alerted companies to their legal requirements and the need to protect staff from undue stress. Companies which fail to take reasonable care of the health and welfare of their employees will be particularly vulnerable to such litigation.

That's possibly why more companies are becoming aware of the benefits of offering Employee Assistance Programmes or EAPs. You may recall my colleague Andrew Walton, the consultant psychologist who helps passengers overcome their fear of flying. Andrew is also a leading EAP specialist. This service gives staff access to trained counsellors with whom they can discuss their problems. The problem doesn't have to be a work-related one and staff are free to discuss any issue in total confidence. Obviously the presence of a qualified professional can greatly assist you if you are experiencing stress. You may be fortunate enough to work with a company that operates such a scheme, or if you are thinking of moving job it's worth finding out what their health and safety policies are.

If you are experiencing stress in the workplace and there is little if anything on offer from your employers, make a commitment to yourself to do something about it. When companies don't co-operate you may have to be the one who takes the initiative. Protesting privately or internalising the situation does not help to move you forward. There are steps you can take to coach yourself through an unsatisfactory working environment. Just by being aware that you are experiencing stress can contribute to alleviating some of the symptoms. There are factors that you can control and control allows you to make choices.

Some jobs are obviously more stressful than others by the very nature of the work involved, and the pressure that goes with those jobs is part of the daily routine. Working under pressure is not necessarily harmful: you may find it a positive thing and work better that way. The problems arise when you exceed the level of pressure you can cope with and your mental and physical health suffer in the process.

Most people find it very difficult to express dissatisfaction without it leading to conflict. And many people suffer in silence for fear of conflict. This can be a good time to practise your skills of communication. Recalling the techniques in Chapter 7, you'll remember that by writing out what you want to say in advance there's less chance of getting side-tracked. Confrontation in the workplace puts you under immense stress. There can be the fear of disapproval, losing your job, reducing your chances of promotion and – equally frustrating – having no voice. A pattern can set in where you are caught up in a cycle of replaying the same events and getting the same outcome.

Linda's reason for wanting to be coached was the constant conflict she was experiencing in her workplace. Linda found it difficult to deal with her boss and just as hard to manage the staff under her. She worked in a busy advertising agency in which deadlines were the norm. She loved the creative element of her work but hated the daily politics.

To coach Linda successfully, it was important to get as much background information about her work situation as possible. The fact that Linda had been promoted to a senior managerial position with no prior training seemed a very relevant factor in her problem communicating effectively with her boss and subsequently delegating to her staff. The focus of Linda's coaching programme was on improving her communication skills.

Using her coaching forms, Linda set the following goals: to enjoy her working day, to improve her relationship with her boss and to learn how to delegate and manage staff. Linda was careful to set positive goals.

In the problem section, Linda wrote 'I am stressed by the constant confrontation with my immediate boss about prioritising work. It upsets me that my team of staff complain about the pressure of deadlines and my mood swings. I have a real problem creating a happy working atmosphere.' By stating her problems this way, Linda avoided blaming other people and relayed how the problems were affecting her. That meant she could put herself in a position to do something about them.

By bringing the problem back to herself, Linda was able to question how her behaviour affected things. Linda got to work on her communication skills. Her boss was inclined to give Linda a job and then during the course of the day to throw something else at her. Linda would drop what she was doing and get to work on another project, only to have her boss kick up a storm because the previous job wasn't finished. Linda's old defensive approach, explaining why it wasn't her fault, didn't work.

Linda could see a pattern: she was doing exactly the same thing with her own staff. Once she appreciated that she was not particularly good at delegating herself she was more tolerant of her boss's inability to delegate and prioritise. The situation began to look less personal.

Linda could now apply the rules of coaching. By adopting a new approach she could coach the boss and her staff. The first thing was to stop conforming to and repeating negative patterns of behaviour. Assume that Linda's boss has formed the opinion that Linda is incompetent. Why? Because she never finishes a job on time. The boss may be totally unaware that he has set this situation up. Nevertheless a pattern has been set which leads to the same old confrontation.

Linda decided to break this pattern. And it really wasn't difficult. Linda used time to monitor the deadlines. Every job came with the 'urgent, urgent' request. So Linda asked for a completion time. Initially she got a response of 'as soon as possible', but she persevered. Without provoking confrontation, she requested a specific time, reassuring her boss that she didn't want to let him down. When a new job was thrown at her, Linda gave her boss the option of which one he would like her and the team to give priority to. By concentrating on prioritising her own time, Linda was able to help her boss prioritise the work, without his even realising it. A few weeks later, Linda's boss even complimented her on the smooth running of her division.

When negative patterns set in at work, negative assumptions are often made. Linda had assumed that her boss didn't like her and was deliberately putting her down. Perhaps he was under pressure from an ineffective boss further up and a negative pattern was being repeated down the line. Either way, what made the difference to Linda's working environment was by taking responsibility for the part she played. Of course, the workplace is a hotbed for all kinds of human relationships, and there may be personal issues at play. But getting caught up in personal issues hardly leads to progress being made. Will the assumption that your boss is a tyrant, and the staff impossible, change the situation for you? Of course not. These are nail-in-the-coffin assumptions which only compound the problem. What you are seeking is a workable solution, one that will alleviate your problem. There is a whole bunch of personalities with whom you have to contend in the workplace, and how they respond to you is as much to do with your reactions as it is with theirs. If you want to take control, then, you can't keep passing the power to other people.

While Linda was able to deal with her problem successfully, the situation may never have arisen had the company provided adequate training. However skilled you are at your job, that is no indication that you have the ability to manage others. Training is without a doubt the best option. But what do you do if your company doesn't offer management training? Without realising it, you may well repeat the patterns of an ineffective superior.

There's a scenario I refer to as yelling down the ranks. It goes like this: the managing director yells at his fellow directors, who then yell at their senior managers, who in turn yell at divisional managers, who yell at the supervisors, who yell at the rest of the staff. But in fact all the trouble was caused by the MD losing his temper. The one complaint that really gets to me, is the one in which the people in charge point the finger of blame at the staff. So if I were asked 'How do you get good staff?' my standard reply would be 'Create an environment that allows them to be good.' You can see how the approach I take does not appeal to all bosses. Heaven forbid the problem should lie with them.

Don't think I'm letting you off the hook with that one. You see, the essence of coaching is to look at yourself first. Trying to find someone else to blame slows down the whole process. You can't change your life if you keep passing the buck. Some situations are out of your control. If good staff training is not part of the culture of your workplace you have to find a way of dealing with it. Leaving your present employment is not always a feasible option. Only you know the consequences this would involve. But – and this is perhaps a more important point – if you remain unaware of the part you play, old problems can follow you into a new working environment.

Whenever I've done coaching within a company structure, I've always found that staff welcome the opportunity to talk about other issues as well as work-related ones. Sometimes it can be a bit of a battle convincing employees of the relevance of tackling other issues. But, as I hope you will know by now, I firmly believe that you can't separate out the different areas of your life. They all have a significant effect on each other. When it comes to work and career you have to define the relevance along with the importance of this to your life.

▪ Means and Ends Goals

As with any other goals, work goals can be seen as a means to an end. Your goal may be to have a job with the ultimate aim of financial security. In fact, finances could be your most significant aim. The bit in the middle, i.e. the work you do, may be less important, and job satisfaction may not be the end goal you have set. But because work accounts for a great deal of your time you need to be sure about what your Means and Ends goals are in this area. Can you contend with a boring job? And will the pay cheque be adequate compensation? Are the demands made on your time affecting your physical and mental well-being? Is the end enough to justify the means? Give this some thought when you set work and career goals. The end goal may look very attractive, but as you're the one carrying out the bit in the middle, are you sure you've made the right choice?

▪ Creating the Perfect Job

Some jobs sound great, don't they? I bet you can think of a few you fancy doing. A friend of mine likes the idea of becoming a pilot, walking through the airport in a smart uniform, travelling to exotic locations and announcing over the tannoy: 'This is your pilot speaking.' There's only one small problem – he hates flying. So sometimes there is a pretty valid reason for your dream job not becoming a reality. Having said that, there may be less to stop you going after the career you really want than you think.

You may have a very idealistic view of a particular job. Without a doubt, some do appear very glamorous on the surface, but having worked with clients from a range of professions that goes right across the board, I can tell you that, regardless of their particular job, their problems are not that dissimilar. All types of work involve interpersonal relationships and while some professions are more people-oriented than others, you will nearly always be dealing with people, be they clients or fellow workers. Every job has some form of pressure or stress to it and, with more companies downsizing, longer working hours for the most part are on the increase. Where the major problems tend to occur are: break-downs in work relationships, e.g. with a boss, or colleague, or clients; demanding workloads and excessive working hours; lack of enjoyment, job satisfaction, mental stimulation and overall fulfilment.

These problems can be found in just about any profession. They can exist in isolation or you can experience them all. And just because you experience them is by no means an indication that those around you will too. However, if you think that problems are isolated to your particular workplace, it might come as a nasty shock when you move and experience them elsewhere. It's not as if you are likely to be expecting a problem-free working environment to start with, but you probably think it would be nice to have got away from that poisonous atmosphere you lived in before. You will be in a better position to strike that balance when you are clear about the main advantages your job has to offer. Work through the technique below to get a detailed picture of what you are after.

EXERCISE

1. Imagine your ideal job. Now, write it down in as much detail as possible, i.e. what exactly does the work entail, what will you be doing, what are your working hours, what's the salary, what type of benefits are offered, e.g. pensions, private health insurance, training, company car etc.

2. Imagine you are interviewing someone for that job. Prepare a detailed questionnaire and application form and specify relevant qualifications. What sort of experience would the candidate require? What sort of person are you looking for?

3. Fill in your questionnaire and application form. Include your CV.

4. Did you give yourself the job?

If you did, well done. If you didn't get the job, how could you get it the next time? What development skills, training, qualifications, experience or further information do you require?

If you are serious about getting the right job you need to have a plan of action. As with all your goals, wanting them isn't enough. You can begin by gathering as much information as possible about the job that you have in mind. Remember that information allows you to make informed decisions and extends the choices you have.

▪ Work and Career Form

If you want to make any changes to your Work and career form, now is the time to do it. Here are some more examples of the sort of things to include for each section.

Goals
- Improve my performance
- Increase my product knowledge
- Build better relationships with clients and colleagues
- Become a team player
- Be more selective about the work I take on
- Find a better-paid job
- Increase my knowledge of the marketplace
- Get promotion in the next six months

Personal strengths
- I'm determined
- I'm a self-starter
- I'm hardworking
- I'm enthusiastic
- I'm motivated
- I'm willing to learn

Immediate challenges/blocks/problems
- My job is boring
- I'm not very good at organising myself
- I find it hard to say no and as a result take on too much
- I allow myself to be easily undermined
- I find the constant pressure very stressful
- My motivation/morale is low

Development skills
- Learn to relax and switch off
- Improve my sales skills
- Improve my communication skills
- Take some additional courses, e.g. a computer course, or sales training, presentation training etc
- Work on having a positive approach and not get caught up in negative office politics/gossip

Achievements
- Good sales figures
- Recent promotion
- Good reputation
- Good time-keeping and conduct record
- Excellent references

Go through your own form and make sure everything is in the relevant category so that there are no problems in the goal section; keep problems specific to you and how they affect you; identify your strengths, not your weaknesses; make sure you have included development skills (as many as you can please) and the same goes for achievements. If you overload your form with problems and don't give enough emphasis to the other sections you'll find it difficult to move forward.

Once you have some goals in place, the next step is to set a time frame for achieving them. Don't leave it open-ended or the goals will remain out of reach. With a time frame you can now work on a plan of action. Include in your plan all the ways that you can contribute to your goal on a regular, ideally daily, basis. With development skills, set a time frame and action plan, so for example if your future development skill is to take a computer course, your first plan of action may be getting information on the type of courses on offer, the cost and the length of time they take. Then you need to enrol on a course and make a commitment to complete it. You now have an action plan and time frame for acquiring your new development skill. There is no point in being aware of the areas you can improve on if you don't follow through.

▪ Conclusion

▶ If you are experiencing too much stress, work on ways to reduce it.

▶ Find out if your company offers any provisions for dealing with stress that you would benefit from.

▶ If you are in the process of looking for a new job, get as much information as possible about how family/staff-friendly the company is. Do they meet your needs?

▶ Don't repeat negative behaviour patterns that keep you locked in a dispute.

▶ Be clear about your means and ends goals.

▶ Create the perfect job.

▶ Review your form and make sure you have a time frame and plan of action.

CHAPTER ELEVEN

Finances

MANY PEOPLE HAVE a problem stripping down finances. By that I don't mean reducing your finances, but simply taking a close look at what they are and how far you expect them to go. I'm not a financial adviser, I'm a coach, and while I can coach you to manage your finances and even improve your earning potential, I can't coach those few more pennies out of your piggy bank. And for every client whose earning potential has been increased through coaching there are clients who have willingly reduced their earning potential. Why? Because they have chosen to do something that they actually enjoy, and which therefore offers them something that money alone cannot offer.

I don't see coaching as some get-rich-quick scheme, not if your definition of riches is based on money. Like every other area of your life chart there is no universal scale as to how much money is enough. Most people go through life convinced that no matter how much they've got, it's never enough. I say this with some confidence because I've coached several millionaires. And believe it or not, the same old issues keep coming up.

▪ Where to Start

You need to start, obviously, by looking at your finances, and forgive me if we go back to basics, but you'd be amazed at the number of people who seem determined not to get the simple things right! Do a few crude calculations as to what you have coming in each month and what you have going out. It helps to keep bills because some arrive quarterly and you can work out the monthly average. Check your credit card statements; look out for things like your limit increasing. Do the same with bank statements: is your overdraft going up, are you constantly juggling with money coming in and money going out? Are you managing to save money? Divide your outgoings into the following categories: necessary expenditure, which includes mortgage/rent; amenities i.e. gas, electric, service charges; food; travel expenses; hire purchase payments; standing orders. In your other list include all the expenses that are not crucial or necessary ones. So your list could include clothes, entertainment, recreational habits, e.g. smoking, drinking, buying the latest car, CD player, fashion accessory. You will probably find it difficult to know what category to put some items in because a particular purchase will seem like a necessity. But be really honest about how crucial it is, because if you are looking to find ways of reducing your outgoings, you need to establish what the really necessary ones are, and the best way to do that is restrict the list to two categories (necessary and non-necessary). That way you can see how much disposable income you have left before you decide whether or how to spend it.

There's no point repeating the same old patterns if they involve you chasing your tail every month. If you are in control of your existing finances you can start setting some goals. On the other hand if you are not you need to get them in order before moving on. As always it helps to have information. If your finances have got seriously out of control, don't ignore them, get help. This can be anything from talking to your bank manager to consulting a financial adviser or even contacting the Citizens' Advice Bureau, which is a free service. Doing nothing will only lead to more trouble.

There are also some simple applications you can get in the habit of doing, like filling in the stubs in your chequebook and making a note of your expenditure on a daily basis. That way you won't open your purse or wallet and wonder where all the money went. Or have the embarrassment of having your credit card refused. I know some very high-earning individuals who had to face that dilemma. It's a very simple rule: if you take out more than you put in, the well will run dry. So it's up to you to know how much you are taking out.

You may be wondering about joint finances, especially if you share an account with a partner who likes to spend. The basic response is be sensible and don't make things worse than they already are.

Julie, one of my clients, was fed up with her husband's reckless attitude to money because every month the bank statement showed that he had again put their account into the red. Julie was horrified by the ridiculous and extravagant purchases. 'Why does he have to insist on paying for everyone when he goes out, when he knows we can't afford it?' Julie asked me. As you know, the wrong questions won't move you forward. And like you I don't have a crystal ball that gives me some insight into what makes people do what they do. Even if you did know, it won't necessarily change the situation, whereas asking the right questions will.

During our coaching session, I suggested to Julie some useful coaching questions, such as 'How can I change this situation?' and 'How can I make it work for me?' Once Julie had asked those questions, she soon had a sensible answer, which was not to have all her finances going into a joint account. Julie's husband John wasn't only being reckless with his finances, he was also being reckless with hers. When Julie studied their finances more carefully, she was startled to discover that she was paying all the bills, either through direct debit or standing order. Her husband was treating his salary like disposable income and dipping into what was left of Julie's salary.

As you can imagine, Julie had a few issues to tackle in her relationship chart, but in the mean time she was determined not to let the financial pressure continue. Julie paid her share of the household expenditure into the joint account, dispensed with her joint credit card and kept her own separate account. Things did get a bit hairy over the next few months. The phone got cut off and John had his credit card refused when he tried to pick up the bill for dinner. But Julie wouldn't budge and refused to pay for the phone reconnection or to clear John's credit card. John was the one with the problem, not her, and she wasn't going to finance his excessive lifestyle. Finding a solution is far from easy at any time, but Julie stuck to her guns and eventually her husband had to address his overspending. He kicked up a storm in the process, although Julie could see that doing nothing only allowed John to indulge in his bad habit of overspending. It was important for Julie to feel in control of her own finances before dealing with the issues in her relationship.

As you can see, boundaries come into play on many levels. Julie had put some very clear boundaries in place by stopping her husband having access to all her finances. Julie can't see a time in the immediate future when she would trust John enough to share an account as they had before. But he has curbed his spending and she is optimistic about their future together. As well as setting boundaries, it was important to coach Julie to take control of the situation.

▪ More to Lose

To a certain extent I guess the more you have the more you have to worry about losing. And that's the cycle many individuals seem stuck in.

Take for example a client of mine called Peter, a successful freelance surveyor who had moved house three times in six years. When I asked him why, I got the answer, 'Well that's what people do in my position, and as a surveyor I've got a real advantage in choosing the right property. Every property I've bought I've sold for almost double what I paid for it.' Now that sounds like a pretty shrewd investment, until he told me that his mortgage hadn't gone down, it had gone up because each new property he bought was so much more expensive than the previous one. Perhaps Peter could realise the capital in his property if he sold it, but it gave Peter no added personal security. On a daily basis he was battling with the high mortgage and all the other outgoings that he had added to his list like holidays, cars, school fees and so on.

Peter wanted coaching because he had many sleepless nights worrying about his finances. No matter how much money he earned he was always struggling to keep his head above water. At times, he said, it felt like little had changed since his student days, when he was battling with a limited budget and constant overdraft. Whilst clients are quick to see a pattern they all too often prefer to hand over the responsibility of dealing with it, prompting complaints from Peter along the lines of: 'I'm just hopeless when it comes to money.' What I said to Peter applies to all my clients: it's one thing to recognise your failure to manage your finances to date, but you have to be careful about sweeping statements that keep you where you are.

It would seem that regardless of what Peter earned, the pattern remained the same. There's no great mystery about it; Peter was living beyond his means. In fact he was putting himself under a lot of unnecessary pressure, and the only way for Peter to release that pressure was by accepting that it really was self-imposed.

Peter decided not to move, and to monitor his finances a lot more closely. His existing home was beautiful, so why not enjoy it? When he discussed it at length with his wife, he discovered that she wasn't that keen on moving anyway. Peter's wife had assumed, because she had never been informed to the contrary, that finances were not a problem and that Peter knew what he was doing. When Peter shared his concerns with her, along with the true state of their finances, she was baffled as to why on earth he had contemplated moving again. She was even more baffled by his reply which was 'I thought it was what you wanted.'

Amazing, isn't it, the assumptions you make along the way, especially as far as money is concerned. However the only way to move forward in coaching is bring those assumptions back to yourself. Peter might have been working on some instinct or hunch that caused him to make that assumption, but ultimately he was making his own judgement.

As you can see in the case of Peter, coaching encouraged him to take the responsibility of monitoring his own finances, and communicate the true state of his finances to his wife. Involving her in the discussions took a lot of pressure off Peter by allowing him to hear what his wife really felt about the situation, rather than living beyond his means because he had assumed his wife wanted more.

While I'm all for setting goals in your financial chart and having a healthy attitude to your value, the wrong goals will restrict you and stop you enjoying what you already have.

Clearly the issue of finances has more to it than just knowing one's way round a calculator. No doubt that's why many of my clients are accountants or city analysts, all of whom have financial problems or worries. It's amazing, isn't it, that accountants can prepare cash flows that would bamboozle the average person, and yet they are still capable of spending beyond their means and worrying about money.

No matter how much you earn, the issue of money can become relative, and result in your being stuck in the same cycle. If you live in a bedsit your goal might be to have a one-bedroom flat, and once you've got that you want a house, then a garage, then a garden and a maybe a pool would be nice. So on and on it goes and, if you're not careful, you won't even enjoy the latest upgrade, you'll be too busy going after what you haven't got.

Regardless of what others think of you, you can only feel inadequate with your own consent. So if you think you haven't got the right house, the right car, the right job or the right clothes, you are the one with the casting vote. And if you want to have control of your finances and make them work for you, it makes sense to have your priorities in place.

When you set goals in your financial chart, you need a logical way to go about achieving them. The time scale does make a difference in this area. Don't treat these goals like lottery numbers – listing them won't automatically produce the finances you need to achieve them.

A story I like to tell at this stage concerns a friend of a friend who inherited a large house in the centre of London. When it came into her hands the area was pretty drab, but within five years, every restaurant-owner in the country seemed to be camping out on the streets to try and get a site, and she realised she was sitting on a lot of money. When she had done it up, it sold for – deep breath – just over £2 million. As the deal neared completion, she was phoning my friend every day and each time she sounded more distressed. 'Will I have enough to retire on? What if I get bored not working? What if property prices go up even higher?' All that sort of thing. By the end of the month my friend had run out of patience and decided to tell her friend to get things in perspective. 'Listen,' she said, 'I'm sitting here trying to work out if I've got enough money to pay for postage stamps, and you're asking me if £2 million will see you through retirement. What can I say, you can buy a hell of a lot of stamps for £2 million.'

Attitude will affect a lot of the issues you have with finances. It isn't pleasant to go through life wondering if you will ever have enough money, and yet many people who don't need to do just that. You'd be much better placed if you had a few ground rules in place and some clear ideas about where you are going with your finances. Try answering these questions in your journal.

► How much money would be enough?

► Am I happy with my current financial status?

► What are the major problems I face? (List them.)

► What am I doing to change/improve the situation?

► Do I work to a monthly budget?

► Am I planning for the future, i.e. pensions schemes, life insurance, and savings?

► Am I spending beyond my means?

► Can I see any patterns in my financial status?

► Do I enjoy my money?

► What changes am I prepared to make to my standard of living?

After looking at that list – and before you go through the financial form – you'll really want to get your financial house in order or make a commitment to doing so. Unless you take control of this area it's easy to set goals like making more money, having a bigger house, getting a new car. There's nothing wrong with these goals, but if finances are a problem, you could be pursuing all the things that previously caused you trouble. A more appropriate goal could be taking control of your finances and staying in credit. So take a few minutes to assess what your current financial status is like before you move on.

▪ Knowing your Value

When I was filming the documentary for the Millionaires series, the interviewer asked me how much I was worth. It's a common enough question; in fact you often hear people talk about some-one's value in terms of finances. What I can tell you is that my financial status at that time couldn't have bought peace of mind at any price. And in my experience money alone is never enough to compensate when other areas of your life are out of balance. I'm sure some of you will be saying it must help all the same. But it's not always the case. When you're running a business a lot of your value is tied up in that business and if a dispute takes place the dynamics quickly change. Money often becomes the issue that controls the resulting power struggle. And in many work situations money is used to make you toe the line.

When you are in an unsatisfactory work situation you can't simply get up and walk out, especially when you need the money. This takes place on all levels of earnings. For the most part, high earners have high overheads that have to be met. Leaving behind a high salary means you have to let go of something, which can be a way of life, possessions, or your home. Letting go isn't easy: after all, you must have worked hard to get where you are and, when your finances become threatened, it's like having the carpet pulled from beneath your feet.

You may not realise how important your finances are to you until they are put under threat. Panic quickly sets in and you'll find yourself desperately trying to hold on to what you've got – that's certainly what I did. In reality your attention can be so firmly fixed on staying where you are that you're probably not even looking. But there are times in life when the best way to move forward is simply to let go, and it comes down to knowing your true value. If you place your value around financial wealth, you might find that you have been holding on too tightly to something that doesn't make you happy. In fact, it could be making you very unhappy.

Finances are often high on people's value list. To a lot of people they are the most visible, tangible expression of a person's security. It's an obvious link and yet, regardless of financial status, you might not enjoy that security. The question you probably haven't explored is 'What would it take for me to feel secure?' When you answer that question, leave finances aside for the moment. Instead examine the others areas of your life chart, for example:

- ▸ **Health** Would an annual medical check-up make you feel secure about your health?

- ▸ **Spiritual and Religious** Would a strong belief and commitment make you feel secure in your faith?

- ▸ **Work and career** Would a supportive boss make you feel secure in your work?

- ▸ **Personal relationships** Would a loving partner make you feel secure in your relationship?

- ▸ **Family/extended family** Would a supportive family make you feel secure?

- ▸ **Friends/social life** Would a stimulating social life and loyal friends make you feel secure?

I'm sure most of you believe that money isn't everything. But if you really want balance in your life you have to question your relationship to money and how much your life really hinges on it. Just as money can allow you to enjoy the finer things in life, it can also stop you when it dictates every decision you make. You are interactive in every area of your life and if one area is out of balance it can affect all the others. Finances have to be kept in perspective. When you value all seven areas it will affect the decisions you make. Knowing what's really important to you and what you truly value puts you in a position to make the right decisions and, if necessary, let go of something.

How does letting go apply to your financial dealings? It's really a question of letting go of the fear that controls many people's lives. Fear blocks your progress and prevents you from moving forward. In my own case, when I let go of the fears and tensions that had been taking me over, my financial situation didn't get worse, it got better. And the reason it got better was not because my bank balance doubled but because I had total control over it. Yes, it could have gone either way and you have to be aware of that. But when you appreciate that your life is worth more than your financial value it will give you the courage to move forward. So if I was to be asked the question again 'How much are you worth?' I'd say a lot more than I used to be.

Now you can return to the question of 'What would make you feel secure financially?' Be specific, as it will help you set appropriate goals.

▪ Finance Form

Goals
- Start a pension plan
- Save up for a holiday
- Work to a monthly budget
- Increase my earnings
- Save £100 per month

These goals are bringing something you want. Like every other section you may be initially inclined to list what you don't want, for example: stop overspending; stop feeling under pressure to keep up with everyone else; stop my partner overspending. Don't list those things here. Keep negative goals for the problem section.

Personal strengths
- I always monitor my finances
- I'm very disciplined and good at saving
- I never spend beyond my means
- I'm very generous with friends and never mean with my money
- I enjoy my money
- I have a pension scheme, saving fund etc.
- I earn a very good salary

Immediate challenges/blocks/problems
- I overspend and end up in debt
- My overheads are very high
- Clients never pay me on time, which affects my cash flow
- I'm always trying to keep up with friends, which leads me to overspend
- I don't earn enough money
- My work situation is insecure

Break your problems down as you work through them. So if you feel you don't earn enough money, write down how much would be enough, then move on to asking the right questions, such as 'How can I change things? What can I do to improve the situation? How would I relieve the pressure?'. Don't hit a wall with your problems. If you find yourself coming up with 'There's nothing I can do', refer back to Part 1 of this book. You need to keep in the right frame of mind to find a solution. Also remind yourself of your value list and what's really important to you.

Development skills
- Learn to monitor my finances
- Get some financial advice
- Be less concerned about keeping up with others
- Get some information on various savings schemes

Achievements
- My house is paid for
- I have no debts
- I have savings
- I've invested my money wisely
- I've learnt to let go and be less concerned about finances

When you fill in your form, keep it consistent with the focus on the goals you have set. You are looking for personal strengths to support your goals, development skills to achieve them, and achievements that boost your self-confidence.

▪ Setting a Value

Earlier in the chapter the issue of value was more to do with a personal value. So let's look at your financial value and how much your time is worth. One thing is for sure: whatever value you place on yourself, not everyone will agree with it. We all have our personal scale of values, be they for services, property, cars or other possessions. When you walk into a shop to purchase something your mental calculator has its own scale as to what is an acceptable price to pay. And depending how much emphasis you place on something, that scale probably varies greatly. My sister loves to buy expensive make-up, but can't get her head round how much I spend on shampoo.

You'll be well aware that certain occupations command a particular salary, but as most people accept, there can be salary variations within the same company for what amounts to the same job. In the service sector in particular, prices vary enormously. Why? Because some people place a higher value on what they do and customers are prepared to pay for it. You may subscribe to the principle you get what you pay for and if you're happy with what you've got there's no problem.

However, the psychology of how people relate to money is baffling. Manufacturers know that if some goods are priced too cheaply the consumer assumes they're low quality. Price them too high and you could exclude your target market. Getting it just right is not easy, especially when it comes to setting your own value. There are no hard and fast rules for you to use, and it will also depend on your profession. Only you can truly know what you're comfortable with and believe you deserve. What I can tell you is this, that regardless of what level you are pitching at, there will always be those who question your value, so don't be disheartened and think it only happens to you. Just because some people question your value, it doesn't mean you are worth less.

When it comes to placing a financial value on yourself, you are worth exactly what you believe you are worth, or – I should say – are prepared to accept. You have to know your bottom line. There's a fine line between selling yourself on the basis of what you have to offer and feeling that you have to justify your value on every level. Take my advice and don't opt for the second option. If your are in a situation and you feel that your value is being undermined, use this golden rule that has served me well: 'No one can make you feel inadequate without your own consent.' It's easy to keep blaming other people for having an issue with money when in fact all they are doing is reflecting some of your own anxieties over money issues.

You have to be comfortable with the value you set for yourself, otherwise you'll always feel compromised. The first thing I always tell perspective clients is my fee, and if this is a problem I make them aware of other coaches who charge considerably less, so they can make a choice. Even if they have questioned my fee, which is non-negotiable, I have no problem telling them about the service I offer. You see, while they may have an issue with my fee, I don't.

I once had a barrister contact me who was interested in being coached. At the end of our conversation and after asking me lots of questions he said, 'I must say, I think you're terribly expensive.' To which I replied, 'I must say, I don't. I'm completely comfortable with the fee I charge and the value I place on my time.' The issue of the fee wasn't my issue, it was his. By the way, a week later he called me back and became a client, but that's another story.

▪ Conclusion

► Take a close look at your finances. You need to know exactly what they are and how far you expect them to go.

► Watch out for repetitive patterns, e.g. your finances may have increased over the years and yet you are still battling with an overdraft.

► A joint bank account is only practical when both parties behave responsibly.

► It's up to you to take control and responsibility for your finances.

► How much money is enough? Before you set goals in your financial chart, you need to consider this question. If you don't know, it's easy to become stuck in a cycle of continually pursuing more, with no ultimate goal in mind.

► When it comes to placing a financial value on yourself, you are worth exactly what you believe you are worth.

CHAPTER TWELVE

Personal Relationships

THE FOCUS OF THIS chapter is to coach you through close personal relationships. You're already an expert in this area and if you don't believe me you soon will. You know exactly what you need in a relationship, but when emotions come into play many people's theories go flying out of the window. Out of all the areas that you will coach yourself through, you may find this one the most difficult to play the role of detached spectator when seeking a solution to a problem. Let me reassure you by saying that the techniques in this chapter don't ignore the issues at stake. If anything, the focus is on resolving problems that perpetuate your emotional pain and keep you stuck with it.

If you are not in a relationship you will find this chapter equally useful as the techniques may help you come to terms with old relationships, break negative patterns and bring into your life the sort of relationship you are looking for.

▪ Get in Touch with What You Want

For the purposes of this chapter, I would like you to work on your forms by yourself, to begin with. You may feel you would prefer to do them with your partner, and it's true that it makes sense to have joint goals. At this stage, though, you need the space to get in touch with what you want and when emotions are involved it's easy to be influenced into pursuing a goal you may not truly desire. Deep down you do know what you want, but fear can suppress it and what you may fear the most is the consequence of pursuing it.

A few years ago 1 was having dinner with a group of friends in a restaurant. The evening was going well and everyone seemed in good spirits, until the subject of holidays came up. The couple sitting next to me couldn't agree on a suitable holiday location that would satisfy both of them.

Geoff made a number of suggestions to his girlfriend Tanya, all of which she rather brutally rebuffed. The atmosphere soon became strained and, despite the efforts of the rest of the party to steer the conversation on to another subject, Geoff and Tanya became locked into a heated dispute.

For a few minutes we all tried to ignore them, hoping they would resolve their differences. Eventually someone at the table waved an arm between them and said, 'Time out, you two.' Geoff broke off in mid-sentence and with a note of surprise in his voice. 'We're not arguing, we're just trying to come to an agreement on where to go on holiday,' he said.

His girlfriend interrupted, 'And the only reason we can't agree is because Geoff won't listen to anyone.' Encouraged by the attention of an audience, Tanya launched into a narration along the lines of 'The trouble with Geoff is . . .'. If you have ever witnessed a couple arguing in public I'm sure you will agree that there are better ways to spend an evening.

Geoff's response at being the subject of a public tongue-lashing was to storm off to the men's room. Tanya shook her head in disbelief. 'See what 1 mean?' she sighed, looking around for support. Her comments were met with silence and most of us lowered our eyes to the table, waiting for the moment to pass.

As 1 was sitting next to Tanya, she turned her attention to me. 'What do you think, Eileen?' she said, a little louder than 1 would have preferred. Feeling 1 had no choice but to reply, 1 said 'As 1'm not the person going on holiday with you, 1 think it's more important what Geoff thinks.'

When Tanya finally resumed the conversation with Geoff, it turned out that the break he had in mind was a permanent one. Tanya learned a very painful lesson that evening.

You may have your own set of rules when it comes to the relationship game, but attempting to score points in public can put you out of the game completely. Maybe you think Tanya got her just desserts? Had you been in Geoff's position would you have done the same thing? One thing that I can tell you is that I've never witnessed Tanya behave that way towards a friend. So here's a question that requires a really honest answer; have you ever treated a loved one in a way that you would never dream of treating a friend?

'Yes' would have to be my own answer. And, like me, many couples agonise, despair and suffer feelings of rejection when they discover that the object of their desires has thoughts, feelings, emotions and opinions far removed from their own. When you are in a close relationship you can demonstrate a great deal of synchronicity in your thought processes, but even the strongest of unions can't have the same thoughts at the same time. At the start of any new relationship you are mentally accumulating all the things you have in common that make you so compatible. A relationship counsellor once told me that for the most part your partner retains all the qualities that initially attracted you, and that you spend the rest of the relationship dealing with the things you didn't notice to begin with. How true, I thought.

When you make a decision in your relationship there are always consequences, but taking no action can result in long-term pain, whereas the pain caused by taking action is usually more short-lived. To give you an example: Helen, a client, was desperate to have children. She had been in a relationship for five years and had spent the last two trying to persuade her partner to share her goal. Helen received some alarming advice from friends to go ahead and get pregnant, as her partner would soon get used to the idea. And once the baby was born he'd see things differently and accept the situation. Now that's what I call high override advice. Can you imagine the consequences if that relationship did not go according to plan?

You take a huge risk when you override the feelings of your partner. Not to mention the change in dynamics that takes place when a relationship with two becomes a relationship with three. Helen was not prepared to take the risk and felt it would be wrong to remove her partner's choice. Much as she wanted children, she wanted her partner to want them as much as she did.

When Helen first got together with her partner, she was clear about the fact that she wanted children before she was thirty. Her partner was clear that he didn't. So I guess Helen could have made a decision not to continue the relationship at that point. But it was early days and she was bowled over by her new love. They had so much in common and life was so much more fun with him around. The issue of children wasn't urgent and with a bit of luck he'd change his mind. Five years down the road, he hadn't. So what was Helen to do? Spend a few minutes thinking about how you would coach Helen. As a guideline, hold back on blaming either partner for the situation. Blame will not help to move Helen forward. She has invested five years in this relationship and does not need to be told those years were wasted.

I'd say that Helen has a choice. It is not an easy choice, as she can either stay in the relationship and not have children or end the relationship. Can you see any other choices? Well, she could take the advice of her friends and get pregnant, or she could keep trying to persuade her boyfriend to have children and hope he changes his mind in the future. This is what Helen did: she decided to stay in the relationship. Six months later the relationship was not going too well. Helen found herself constantly picking faults with her boyfriend, and bickering and arguing over the smallest thing.

At the end of the day, only Helen can choose her own solution. But, as I pointed out to Helen, staying with a situation is hardly a solution, it's just a delay tactic. While coaching will encourage you to make a decision, it was never aimed at forcing you to make one before you feel ready.

Compromise will always come into play in your relationships. Even when goals are shared, it's impossible to predict at what point you or your partner can no longer reach a compromise. Having said that, there are ways to reduce the risk. Relationships are transitional and just as they change, you change in the process. What was once a shared goal may not remain one. You may be able to deal with a situation when you move the goal posts, but what happens when your partner moves them? It's not difficult to see why this is the most delicate area of coaching.

Your goal will not go away and, if the situation doesn't change, feelings of resentment can set in. No matter how much fear you have about dealing with something or making a decision, not dealing with it won't change things. In fact, not dealing with it may make things a whole lot worse. The relationship starts to become corrosive and if you're not eating away at yourself you'll find a way of directing your dissatisfaction at your partner. While there is rarely ever only one solution, there is only one answer – deal with the problem.

▪ Personal Relationships Form

Let's go back to those forms for a moment. How well did you score in this section? Review the chart you completed on page 12. If you scored high – congratulations. What you need to focus on now is keeping that score high and not becoming complacent. Just because you have a high score is no reason not to set goals. If your score is low then take heart, we are going to get to work on improving it.

We will continue by reviewing your goals and see how they are shaping up. If you are finding it difficult to set goals and feel blocked by problems you are experiencing in your present relationship, set that relationship aside for the time being. What you should do now is list the goals for your ideal relationship. Don't allow yourself to start thinking about the likelihood of your partner going along with them. This is your chance to express what you want and need. The following list will get you in the mood.

Goals
- I want a loving and supportive relationship
- I want to be loved unconditionally
- I want to get married and have children
- I want to feel equal in my relationship to my partner
- I want to recapture the love we once had
- I want to communicate better with my partner
- I want to find my soul mate
- I want to have more fun in my relationship
- I want to improve the level of trust in this relationship

As always, make sure your goals are positive and talk about what you want to bring into your life. Obviously relationships involve more than one person, but resist the temptation to set goals that involve controlling another person or making them responsible for your goal, such as:

- Make my partner pay me more attention
- Make my partner listen to me and understand me
- Make my partner want children as much as I do
- Make my partner less dependent on me

You'd be surprised by the number of times the word 'make' is used in this section, so be careful not to set goals that involve changing or controlling another person's thoughts and behaviour. Close relationships require you to think in terms of your partner to a greater or lesser extent, based on the commitment of your relationship. What they do not require you to do is think for your partner. There may well be techniques that are aimed at manipulating another person. But personally I do not advocate any method that takes a predatory approach to relationships and disregards issues of honesty or respect for another individual.

Immediate challenges/blocks/problems

You will find it more difficult to keep the problem specific to you in this section, as relationships involve more than one person. However you must define your problem in a manner that allows you to see the part you play in the solution. I'll show you how much difference rewording a problem makes: 'My partner works too much; we never get to spend any time together.'

Now let's say you go off to find a solution for that problem. You might find yourself asking the question 'How can I *make* my partner work fewer hours?' As we've already discussed, it's not appropriate to use the word *make* when it involves controlling another person. You clearly have a problem, which is the lack of time you spend with your partner, so keep your focus on that. Use your journal to write down how the problem affects you. Perhaps it is not possible for your partner to change their working hours, so you may need to look for solutions that help you to deal with the situation. Can you accept the situation? Can you occupy your time in other ways? Is this a major breakdown in your relationship or a temporary blip? Do you ultimately seek a relationship with someone who makes more time for you? Do you think your partner is doing enough to change the situation? Do you feel rejected, taken for granted? Are you putting undue pressure on your partner to change something they have little control over? Stay specific to how the problem affects you and identify what the best possible solution would be. Once you have that in place you can decide how workable it would be.

Now you can address the problem and, if necessary, discuss it with your partner. You want to spend more time with them, and with a bit of luck they feel the same. If you approach the situation carefully there is no need to throw what sounds like criticism at your partner i.e. 'You're always working, you never make time for me.' A better approach is to reinforce your need to spend time with your partner and express your feelings without pushing for a defensive reaction. So, for example, tell your partner you miss having time with them, the children miss them, you're worried about them working so hard and so on. Ask for their input in the solution, and allow them some space to identify the problem for themselves. Work on finding a mutual compromise and avoid issuing ultimatums, which produce defensive reactions. If the approach you have taken in the past has not produced results, be careful not to repeat the same tactics. Be sure that you have looked at all the possible options. Asking for your partner's input can reveal a few more options. Once you feel certain you have explored every avenue you're in a far better position to make a decision.

So let's look at how some other problems could be reworded.

- ► *My partner undermines me*
- ► I allow my partner to undermine me

- ► *My partner won't talk to me/my partner never listens to me*
- ► I need to find ways to communicate better with my partner

- ► *My partner is very moody and always makes me feel it is my fault*
- ► I need to find a way to be less affected by my partner's moods

Remember that if you pass the problem over and make it someone else's, you also pass up the responsibility of finding a solution.

Keep your goal in mind as you work through your mental oasis (as in Chapter 4) to find a solution. To ensure that you are listing problems that relate to this particular section, write down how the problem is getting in the way of your goal, e.g.:

Goal I want a loving and supportive relationship
Problem I'm upset that my partner will not make a commitment to this relationship

The problem identified clearly affects the goal set for this relationship. You can hardly have a loving and supportive relationship when one partner is not committed. That's not to say that you can't achieve your goal, but possibly not in this relationship. You really need to be honest with yourself in this section. Wanting something is not enough, and you can't make a partner commit to a relationship against their will. You can change your goal, but it won't move you forward if you change it to one that allows you to avoid dealing with the real issue. You will find it helps to elaborate on your goal and define what you mean by a loving and supportive relationship and, the clearer you are, the better.

When you have worked through your mental oasis, list the solutions you have come up with. Seeing them on paper will help you to see if they are really workable, rather than just mentally running them by. Obviously it's not enough to have a solution in mind – the tricky bit is acting on it. Because this is such a sensitive area I have included a technique here that I use with clients called 'The Doorway'.

The Doorway

Finding a solution to a problem can involve you making difficult and painful decisions. Only you can decide when you feel ready to do this. Using visualisation techniques can prepare you to move forward.

Write down all the solutions you have come up with. Now close your eyes and imagine that each solution is written on a door. Then stand in front of one of the doors that has a given solution and visualise walking through it. What's waiting for you on the other side? If you don't like what you see, you can step back through the door at any time. Write down in your journal the thoughts, feelings and emotions you experienced. Now do the same for all the remaining doorways.

You can use this technique on a regular basis. You may be surprised how unnerving visualisation methods can be, but they are extremely effective. They will help you to see what it is you really fear from making a particular decision. You will recall in Chapter 5, that when fear is involved negative assumptions are often made. Your brain will predict a negative outcome to the situation. So what you have to do is fill in the missing blanks, by gathering more information and not allowing your imagination to run riot. The more times you enter the doorway the less threatening it looks. When you write down your fears on paper they look less threatening and solutions are more apparent. Keep asking yourself the right questions, e.g. 'How can I make this work for me? How can I turn this situation around? What can I do to change the situation?'. These types of questions keep your brain in solution mode. The Doorway technique allows you to work through your solutions and calm your fears in the process. Just as fear can stop you making a decision it can also push you into making the wrong decision.

As you continue to practise this technique you can become more creative with your visualisation. You can reset the original scene and replace it with a new one. Gaining information helps you to do this. You now have more information about what is stopping you from making a decision and following through with a solution. Solving a problem can involve dealing with several challenges along the way. By recognising what each one is and how it affects you, you have broken the problem down into a series of smaller challenges. You may find it easier to tackle them one at a time rather than hit the problem head on. I'll demonstrate how this works in practice and why you sometimes need to separate cause and effect.

Cause and Effect

Lisa found it difficult to cope with her jealous boyfriend. The situation became so bad that she felt permanently anxious and stressed. If they were out together Lisa dreaded bumping into any men she knew as it always resulted in an interrogation.

Lisa had tried discussing her concerns with her boyfriend, but nothing changed. The only solution that Lisa could see was to end the relationship, the thought of which made her even more anxious and stressed.

Only seeing a black and white solution to a problem can keep you blocked. As Lisa's coach I was concerned about how the problem was affecting her, i.e. the levels of stress and onset of anxiety attacks. This was also a problem that required a solution. So, putting the relationship aside for the time being, we discussed ways in which Lisa could relax and feel less anxious.

Lisa began to break her problem down and see how she allowed herself to be affected by her boyfriend's behaviour. While Lisa believed she gave her boyfriend no cause to be jealous, she was acting as if she was responsible for his behaviour. 'I feel like I'm walking around on eggshells, terrified to put a foot wrong,' was one typical reaction. Lisa had no evidence to suggest she had at any time put a foot wrong. Her boyfriend's behaviour was one problem, but now Lisa had adopted a pattern of behaviour that was causing her a problem.

Lisa decided to deal head on with all the stress and anxiety she was going through. She broke a pattern, which meant that she no longer concerned herself with trying to find a hundred ways to keep her boyfriend happy. She also stopped predicting a disastrous outcome to every date. Lisa reinforced the message by telling herself, 'This is not my fault'.

The transformation was not made overnight. But Lisa's refusal to explain herself all the time, to answer the never-ending questions and to get upset by the ridiculous accusations had an impact, most importantly on Lisa. She no longer felt anxious and upset: she felt angry. Lisa finally found the courage to say to her boyfriend, 'This is not my problem, it's yours, either deal with your jealousy or we no longer have a relationship.' Lisa's boyfriend did not want the relationship to end, so when he decided to go for counselling, Lisa went with him. Lisa had been too taken up with her own situation even to consider this option, which proves that you can control how a problem affects you, but there's no need to take responsibility for a problem that's not yours.

This analogy is more specific to your relationship form than to other areas, because it is so easy to take on the problems of a partner and seek solutions that you are not in a position to implement. You may be in a position to remove the problem, but be careful that you are not seeking solutions to appease somebody else's problem. Be clear about what your problem is and you will find a solution.

Personal Strengths

What are your personal strengths? If you want to have a good relationship, don't you think it's important to be clear about what *you* have to offer? It's amazing how many times I've seen this area left empty by individuals who record a low score. Why do you think that is? Deep down is it that these individuals believe they have nothing to offer, and has their self-esteem reached an all-time low, or do they think it egotistical to identify strengths? Well, dispose of one myth – there's nothing wrong with having an ego. Ego is part of your self-worth, the value you set on yourself. If you want a good relationship you have to believe that you are worthy of one. Otherwise you'll put up with a whole bunch of stuff that you know is unacceptable on the basis that you are not worthy of anything better. In my experience it's more a case of getting what you expect rather than what you deserve. Therefore if you want the very best, set yourself high expectations.

Here are the types of personal strengths that you might list:

- Loyal
- Loving
- Supportive
- Stable
- Faithful
- Sense of humour
- Honest
- Willing to be committed
- Affectionate
- Accepting
- Kind

List as many strengths as you can think of and prepare a list of the sort of qualities you would like a partner to have.

Development skills

Listing future development skills is a great way to see how you can move forward and improve your relationship. You are recognising that it takes two people to create a strong relationship and you are taking responsibility for the part you play. By looking at the problems you have identified, you can see what sorts of development skills are required. So, for example, if you have listed a problem as being poor communication in your relationship, your development skill could be to improve your ability to communicate, listen more, and be less judgemental. The following list will help to get you started:

- Talk more and be more honest about my feelings
- Be more accepting and understanding
- Build my self-esteem and self-worth
- Work on my fear so that I feel less dependent on a relationship
- Stop trying to please everyone
- Stop feeling responsible and trying to fix all my partner's problems
- Learn to set boundaries
- Learn to ask for help/support when I need it
- Learn to be more independent

Achievements

It's easy to take your achievements for granted and not give them the recognition they deserve. But identifying your achievements is crucial to your coaching programme. They serve to remind you how far you have come and boost your self-esteem. It's really not enough to think, 'Well, I've got this far, what next?'. You need to acknowledge what you have achieved, not just mentally but by writing it down. Why? Because it adds to your internal resources and keeps your focus positive. What I don't want you to do is get stuck with your problems and feel weighed down. There may be challenges in front of you, but you have overcome challenges in the past, so don't let them slip your attention. There is a huge emotional pull when it comes to personal relationships and the balance can easily become tilted. All it takes is a few problems: even small ones can tilt the scales. Look deep inside yourself and make your achievement list as long as possible in this area. There may be times when you need to fall back on it and gain the additional strength to move forward.

You can use your current relationship to find achievements and you can also use previous relationships to boost your list. So, for example, if you found the strength and courage to move on from a previous relationship, acknowledge your progress. If you were upset by an old relationship ending, find the positive elements: life did go on; you learnt a lot about yourself in the process; there may have been a mourning period but you went through it and came out the other end.

This may be a good time to review Chapter 3 on developing a positive mental attitude, and read through Marsha's case history again. By asking herself the right questions, Marsha was able to revisit history as opposed to rewriting it. If you are struggling to find achievements you are asking the wrong questions and holding onto the negative. Move yourself forward by asking the type of questions that allow you to focus on what you have achieved, i.e. 'What have I learnt? How have I moved on? What was good about the relationship? What have I gained from the relationship? How would I do things differently the next time?'.

Feelings of hurt can stop you seeing the progress you have made. Here's a thought: focus on the lesson, not the punishment. I like that statement because the harshest punishment is delivered by the 'self' and, however painful the blow, you can increase the pain by turning it in on yourself and mentally delivering the experience over and over again. Your achievement list should far outweigh your problem list, if you are asking the right questions:

► I know what I want

► I'm determined to get it

► I've learnt from previous relationships

► I'm prepared to commit to a relationship

► I know when to get out of a relationship

► I know what I have to offer

► My relationship has come this far

► I have a happy relationship/marriage

► I've learnt a lot about myself in this relationship

► I'm ready to make the necessary changes

► I no longer feel a need to control my partner

► I can be myself in a relationship

► I am less judgmental

► I have children

► I'm prepared to tackle problems in my relationship

► I don't quit when the going gets tough

► I am committed to finding a relationship that's right for me

Some more useful questions to add to your list include: Do I gauge my self-esteem by the state of my relationship? Why do I want this/a relationship? Will this relationship allow me to achieve my goals?

EXERCISE

As a follow-on exercise divide a page in your journal into two halves and draw a vertical line down the middle. On the left-hand side of the page use the heading, 'What is good about my relationship'. On the right-hand side use the heading, 'What is not so good about my relationship'.

When you have completed your list, have a look at the overall balance of your relationship and see how it compares to the score you placed in this section. You may have put a low score, only to discover that there are far more positives than negatives in your relationship. Study your answers carefully. Perhaps you have been holding on to the negative or have given a particular problem more attention than it warrants.

On the other hand you may find that the left-hand list is longer and you are finding more negatives than positives. Does this reflect your score? If not, are you ignoring the true state of your relationship? Ignoring a problem won't make it go away: in fact, the fear of pain that you associate with making a decision can be greater than the consequences of making that decision.

▪ Conclusion

► Acknowledge your own goals in a relationship before working on joint goals.

► Relationships involve more than one person. That's not to say you are responsible for someone else's problem.

► To find a solution to a problem you have to be clear about how it affects you – that effect is something you can control.

► You are not trying to solve other people's problems. To achieve your goals you have to focus on the relevance a problem has to you.

► It's usually easier to find a problem than a goal, so work on finding your true goals.

► Use the 'Doorway' technique when you are finding it difficult to make a decision.

► If you feel weighed down by a challenge, work on your personal strengths, development skills and achievements. The aim is to boost your self-esteem and prepare yourself to make the right decision.

► Refer back to Chapter 3, on positive mental attitude, to keep you in the right frame of mind.

► Use your mental oasis (from Chapter 4).

CHAPTER THIRTEEN

Family and Extended Family

I N THE WORDS OF the old saying, you can choose your friends but not your family. You may have a close relationship with your immediate relatives, but there are times when even this can become strained. As if contending with your immediate family isn't enough, you may also have to adapt to dealing with an extended family. The focus of this chapter is very much on the theme of boundaries: setting your own boundaries and respecting those of other people. With these in place, you will find it a lot easier to resolve existing disputes or problems in this area and avoid unnecessary ones in the future.

Even the most loving parents can risk provoking an angry backlash from their children when they make them feel like they're not being heard. It's only natural for a parent to experience pain when their child is suffering, but as you will see in Sara's story, there are times when you have to allow a family member to express their pain and not overload them with your own pain.

June came to me for coaching with the sole wish of restoring her relationship with her daughter, Sara. In the past, June had always had a close relationship with her, and was therefore upset and dismayed that their relationship seemed to be breaking down at a time when her daughter was going through a painful divorce.

Sara had been devastated to discover her husband was having an affair with another woman. He showed no remorse for the affair and had subsequently moved in with the other woman, leaving Sara and their two year-old daughter. Divorce proceedings were under way, and according to June, Sara was emotionally drained.

When I questioned June on how she saw her role with Sarah, June replied that she was totally supportive of her daughter. She saw her a good deal and they talked a lot on the phone, but she had been baffled by the harsh reaction from her daughter during their most recent telephone conversation. For no reason that June could fathom, her daughter had screamed at her, 'You are so selfish, you never think about anyone but yourself!' How could this be?

To help June through this problem, it was important to start by coaching her into the right frame of mind. June had become blocked by shifting the blame to her son-in-law, and she kept insisting it was his fault that Sara was so distressed.

In order for June to find a solution, she had to be aware of what part she had played in the breakdown of her relationship with Sara. Using the positive mental attitude techniques June was able to diffuse negative emotions that blocked her progress. She also used her mental oasis. Once June was feeling calmer, she explained to me: 'I told her how much I loved her, what a wonderful daughter she is and how she deserved better in life. I said how worried I was, and the number of sleepless nights I was having. Sara said that she cried a lot and felt on the verge of a breakdown. I told her that I felt the same way and had to abandon my weekly shopping, because I burst into tears in the supermarket . . .'

June then paused for a few seconds and said, 'Do you know, I had forgotten just when it happened, but it was as this point that Sara began screaming at me that I was selfish. You can see why I'm so confused, Eileen. I was trying to let Sara know I was also experiencing her pain and she called me selfish.'

I can understand June's confusion, but I can also see why Sara got upset. While it's only natural to experience your own feelings of upset when a loved one is suffering, you have to take care not to overload them with your pain. When you talk about your own pain to someone who is seeking support it can get quite competitive and, once you get locked into your own pain you become unavailable to support the other person.

It had not been June's intention to overload her daughter. But during our conversation she had not identified what the catalyst was for the outburst, only when it occurred. June wanted to give support, so we continued discussing how she could best offer that.

I asked June if she was seeking support from her daughter. She said she wasn't. I then asked her if there was a possibility that Sara found it difficult to hear her mother's upset. June said, 'I've never thought about that although Sara has said to me a few times that she feels guilty and responsible for burdening everyone.'

From a few simple questions, June was able to see that Sara had been worrying. Suddenly the comment 'You're so selfish, you never think about anyone but yourself' made some sense. Although it would be unfair to say it was true, June got a sense of how she sounded to her daughter, and realised it wasn't doing Sara any good to be talking about her own upset. Over the following weeks June made a conscious effort to listen and be supportive. June also acknowledged her own need for support and was able to confide her own anguish to other family members.

Even when family bonds are very close it is risky to assume that you can unload a problem on to the nearest person. But there are times when you need to stand back and review your role. You may be the one called on for support and to fulfil that role your own needs may have to be met elsewhere. The following are useful coaching questions to ask yourself:

- ► How can I express concern and empathy without unloading my own problems?

- ► Do I seek support, or to be supported?

- ► How can I ensure I don't make a person feel worse about the situation than they already do?

- ► Am I talking about my own pain as a means to validate my concern?

▪ Holding on to Hurt

Something I have noticed when listening to clients relaying an upsetting event, and which you may be familiar with, is that the memory becomes selective when it comes to recalling exactly what happened and the sequence of events. When an individual relays what *they* said in comparison to the other person, their inflections and tone of voice are often much softer than seems likely. On the other hand when they speak for the other person they use a much sharper tone of voice. To the listener it can sound like a very one-sided argument, in which the person telling the story was clearly on the receiving end. Obviously this *can* be the case, but I'm sure you will agree that there is usually a trigger point before a confrontation. You can provoke an outburst in someone without deliberately meaning to.

Your emotions override what preceded the attack, especially if you have been criticised or feel insulted. I don't believe people try to distort the truth, but people just do get caught up in a sense of injustice. This can certainly happen with family relationships, when grudges can be held for years after the original outburst.

Maybe because you know your family so well, there is a greater tendency to lash out when you are upset. In fact, it works both ways. Family members can indeed be more forgiving and tolerant of outbursts, but not always. The problems tend to arise when, in the absence of clear boundaries, family members assume it's OK to override the feelings of others on the basis that they are family. Instead of that bond commanding the respect it deserves, for many it warrants little if any respect.

For some families it begins with the children. Obviously a parent will have to make many decisions for a young child, but that's not to say it is appropriate or desirable to ignore the individuality of the child. So, whereas one parent will nurture a child carefully and encourage them through the different stages of growth, another parent may smother the child with too much love, which has the effect of restricting their growth. You have obviously experienced the role of the child and maybe of the parent. Even if your relationship with your parents is a good one, there are likely to have been times when you felt they were forcing their views and opinions on you. As an adult you are in a position to limit any unwelcome interference. Unfortunately, when the lines of communication break down and clear boundaries are not put in place, it can lead to unnecessary conflict. The real problem lies with establishing the boundaries. The resulting conflict is a symptom of the problem and yet that's the place where most people get stuck and emotionally caught up with the problem.

▪ Families at War

Where possible, it is always best to keep disagreements contained to the individuals involved. The problem with family disputes is that's easier said than done. Think very carefully before you involve other family members in your disputes. You may need some validation that you are right, but that's no reason to set off a dynastic feud.

Sue, a client, told me how unpleasant her daughter-in-law was. If only she could make her son see what she was really like. According to her son, his wife could do no wrong and he always took her side. Sue was eager to learn if there were any coaching techniques that could make her son see sense. I asked Sue why she would want to change someone's pleasant perception of a person into an unpleasant one? 'Because his wife is not a pleasant person and I think my son should know the truth about her,' she said defiantly.

She contacted me a few months later. By this time her son was refusing to talk to her and wouldn't answer her calls or letters. She had continued to push the issue of his wife, insisting that his loyalty should be to his mother. He didn't agree. Now she had another problem: her son wasn't talking to her.

Sue wanted to re-establish contact with her son. She had tried apologising but the conversation had gone something like this, 'I'm really sorry I upset you, but I just don't like your wife and I wish you could see things from my point of view.' Now that's a sure-fire way to give an apology with one hand and take it back with the other.

I discussed with Sue some of the more effective ways she could apologise. When she next spoke to her son, she chose to use the apology that particularly appealed to her, which was, 'I'm sorry I upset you, how can I make amends for it?'. She got a very clear response and one that was long overdue. 'Mum,' said her son, 'let's stop fighting. I've picked the right person for me and didn't do it just to please you. I love you but I feel you keep putting that love to the test. You expect me to agree with you on everything and I don't; we're very different people. Alison makes me happy and I love her. That doesn't mean I love you any the less. Just because you don't like her, you expect me to choose between you. I can accept the fact that you don't like her, but you won't let it drop. If you really want to make amends then accept the fact that I'm with her and stop trying to come between us.'

Sue had her answer. Her son loved her and he loved his wife. He had given his mother some very clear boundaries, namely that he refused to let her come between him and his wife. It may not have been what Sue wanted to hear, but at last there was a way out of the impasse. And Sue took it. The funny thing was that once Sue accepted her son's position she started to get on with her daughter-in-law.

▪ How to Say Sorry

It's frustrating when your apologies aren't accepted, but saying sorry doesn't have to be a way of saying you were wrong. You can be genuinely sorry for causing upset although ultimately believe your actions were the right ones. That's the sticking point. Being sorry may not be enough, especially if you are going to continue behaving the same way as before. The lesson to learn from the above case is clear: be careful about putting the word 'but' on the end of your apology. If you want to work through the problems and achieve your goals in your family relationships it is important to establish good communication with family members. This may often involve apologising or compromising (see Chapter 6).

Run these phrases by your mind to see where you are going with an apology. I'm sorry – meaning:

▶ I'm sorry for upsetting you, but this is how I feel and I will continue to stand by it.

▶ I'm sorry for upsetting you: I was wrong to force my opinion on you.

▶ I'm sorry for upsetting you: how can I make amends and put the situation right?

▶ I'm sorry for upsetting you: I formed the wrong opinion.

▶ I'm sorry for upsetting you. I have my opinion, but I will respect yours.

Respecting the opinion of other family members is important, and when it is clear that your view of a person is not shared, it may be appropriate to hold back. There are occasions in coaching when a client is determined to pursue a particular line. As a coach my aim is to steer the client away from unnecessary conflict, but ultimately you are in the driving seat. You control the direction you're going in, and there are usually plenty of warning signs when conflict lies ahead, but still some people choose to ignore them.

In my experience, the biggest fights that take place are internal ones. You can create mental space for people in your life to behave badly, but it takes just as much space to accept that they can behave well. No matter how unpleasant you think someone is, you can be sure that not everyone will see them in the same light. The bullying boss might be perfectly sweet to his wife and children. The office bitch might donate half her salary to charity and always remember to telephone her mother.

There are always people that you choose not to have in your life. The difference with family is that you don't choose it, it's already in place. You can set your own boundaries and you may have to respect those set by other family members. When you fill out your chart for this section it helps to keep that in mind. Families can have joint goals, but for the purpose of this coaching programme we are talking about your goals, not those of others. So let's take a look at your form.

▪ Family and Extended Family Form

Goals
Remember this relates to you and you are setting goals that you are going to achieve which may include:

- See my parents more
- Spend more time with my children
- Improve my relationship with the in-laws
- Have more quality time with my family
- Resolve a difference with my mother/father/sister/brother (other family members)
- Have children

- Talk to my family more
- Give my children a good education
- Be there for my family

Set out goals that are about the things you want to bring into your life, not the things you want to eliminate. You'll make more progress working for a positive goal than a negative one. Here are some examples of negative goals.

- *Spend less time with my family.*
  Make it a positive goal by changing it to:
- Make more time for myself.

- *Stop my family interfering.*
  Make this a positive goal by changing it to:
- Set clear boundaries with my family.

If you are finding it difficult to make a negative goal positive, you may be identifying something that belongs to the problem section. If you find it easier, fill in your problems then go back to your goals.

Goals to avoid are those that relate to other people achieving them e.g.:

- I want my son/daughter to go to college
- I want my parents to get on better
- I want my children to understand the importance of education
- I want my family to be less demanding
- I want my family to accept me
- I want my parents to be more understanding/accepting
- I want my family to appreciate how much I do for them

These may all seem very worthwhile goals, but who do you think is going to achieve them? The onus is not on you, it's on the other people mentioned. I'm not saying they are not goals, but your focus has to be on what you are going to achieve, and therefore that must be your goal. It can and often does include other people, especially in the context of relationships. However, the goal has to come back to you and the rest of your form relates to what's standing in the way of your achieving it. So, let's say your goal is to spend quality time with your family. Your *personal strength* is your commitment to your family, the *problem* is you work long hours.

Your *development skill* is to learn how to say 'No' to extra working hours and your *achievement* is the bond you have with your family. With all that in place, you have a consistent formula, you are setting a goal and working through the 'how' bit, as in 'How can I make a difference? How can I pull on all the resources to make this goal possible?'

You see your goal and visualise the end result. From there, you focus on how to make it happen. If things don't go according to plan, you can work on your running order, which allows you to change the bit in the middle in order to get the end result. You have to put the running order in place. So what I'm asking you to do is make the form work for you. It is not some random sequence of questions; you have to relate them to your situation and make them work for you. Only then can you coach yourself through the situation.

Personal Strengths

Look for personal strengths that help to support your goals and encourage you to overcome challenges. So, for example, if you are having a difficult relationship with in-laws or stepchildren, you can identify that as the problem and a personal strength could be the fact that you are prepared to work on the relationship. You might also identify qualities like being patient, tolerant and accepting of others. Here are few more examples.

- I love children
- I value my family
- I always make an effort to get on with family and relatives
- I'm always there for my family
- I appreciate the importance of having boundaries
- I respect that my family have their own views and opinions
- I can be supportive to my family without getting pulled into family squabbles
- I accept the fact that living up to my own values may not meet the approval of my family

Immediate challenges/blocks/problems

Now you have the chance to talk about what's getting in your way. You don't have to get caught up with what's going on in other people's lives: this is your problem and, if you want to find a solution, keep it specific to you. I know it involves other people, but what I want you to ask yourself is:

- How does it affect me?
- Is this really my problem?
- How can I turn the situation around?
- Am I taking too much responsibility for the situation?
- Am I interfering in an area where I'm not welcome?
- Am I dealing with the problem or the effect the problem is having on me?

Get in the habit of writing down any problems in a way that allows you to feel you have control over them and can influence the outcome. Just rewording a problem can make all the difference and allow you to break it down and find a workable solution. Here is a common problem broken down.

- My family is very demanding and puts huge pressure on me.

Leaving the problem like this may make you feel that you have little control over the situation. You may have protested in the past and not got very far, so it's tempting to think that there is little you can do about it now. Well you can begin by dealing with the effects of the problem – which you can control. You can choose to be less affected by family pressure – sounds too easy doesn't it? Well, ask yourself where the real pressure is coming from. They may be applying pressure on you, but the chances are that you are also putting a lot of pressure on yourself. Somewhere along the line you are taking responsibility for all those demands and all that pressure, and maybe that's part of the problem that you have overlooked. If you have been feeling guilty, that came from within you. Your emotions can feel irrational, but they need permission on your part to gain momentum and continue to exist. So, here are some techniques to help you break the problem down:

1. Make a list of all the ways your family puts pressure on you and makes demands.

2. Divide that list into what you feel is reasonable and unreasonable on their part.

3. At the bottom of each list, write below it something like, 'This is what I'm prepared to take on or deal with' and for the other list write ,'This is what I'm not prepared to take on or deal with'.

4. Using your list, start to write out some boundaries, e.g. 'I will make myself available for the following family functions . . .'; 'I will only take calls at work from family when it is an emergency . . .'; 'I will not constantly keep apologising when I can't do something . . .'; 'When I say no I will stick to it . . .' and so on. The advantage of setting your own boundaries and making the list is that it clarifies in your own mind which things have been causing you problems. If you aren't clear, your family may have been getting mixed signals. Also, when you let things build up and don't deal with them at the time, you are far more likely to get weighed down or have an outburst.

5. If particular family members are more prone to putting pressure on you, write down who they are. Look for patterns: are you constantly giving them the same feedback? Do other family members receive the same treatment as you do? Is their approach always the same? Do they go for the guilt trip? Have they identified your weak spot? Have they just got used to you always being available or doing what they want? Is there an element of predictability in the way the same situations keep occurring?

6. If you are able to see patterns, write them down, see the part you play and list ways in which you can break the pattern.

7. When you have your boundaries in place, think of ways in which you can communicate them. You don't have to present your family with a typed list. Sometimes a simple 'No, I can't do that' will suffice.

This format can be used to break down other problems. It will show you how you can begin by implementing smaller changes rather than trying to deal with the whole problem in one go. If, for example, the whole family becomes involved in a dispute, the problem can seem unmanageable, but when you look closely there are usually just a few family members that are causing the dispute. What you may be experiencing is a chain reaction that requires each part of the chain to be broken down separately in order for you to find a solution.

Development skills

Focus on the kinds of skills you will need to achieve your goals and overcome your problems. Make sure your development skills relate to the other answers in your chart. Here are some suggestions:

- Learn to communicate what I feel without getting angry or upset
- Learn to say no
- Be less affected by family opinions
- Manage my time better
- Learn to listen
- Learn to be more tolerant
- Talk more openly with family
- Ask for support when I need it
- Stop blaming myself
- Make more time for myself
- Stop trying to please everyone
- Work on building my self-esteem
- Accept myself
- Accept others
- Stop feeling responsible

You can use this section to reinforce some affirmations to yourself. So if in the past you have struggled to accept yourself, write out the affirmation 'I love and totally accept the person I am'. Put it in your journal and read it every day. Work on building your strengths. You no longer have to stay stuck with the same old problems when you are equipped with a whole new set of development skills.

Don't forget about gathering information for your file. There may be a particular book or article in a magazine that throws some light on your situation. You might want to talk things over with a professional, or see a course advertised that you would benefit from. Be on the look out for any information that will help to move you forward.

Achievements
You should have the hang of it by now, so don't go holding back on your achievement list. You need to keep reminding yourself of your progress. Add to your achievement list as often as possible. There may be setbacks along the way, so keep them in perspective by weighing them up against what you have already achieved.

▪ Conclusion

► Set positive goals that relate to you and involve you achieving them.

► You may have aspirations for family and children, but remember they also have their own goals and will not necessarily share the ones you have for them.

► Set yourself clear boundaries. It's up to you to be clear about what is acceptable to you. If you aren't clear, how can others be?

► Respect the boundaries of other family members. Be careful not to impose your views on others just because they are family.

► If you decide on a solution to a problem, be prepared for the consequences. The solution may be right for you but that's not to say it will gain the approval of the family.

► Break your problems down. Get in the habit of writing them out in a way that allows you to feel you have control of them and can make a difference.

► You don't have to take responsibility for everyone else's problems. Be aware of when you are putting yourself under unnecessary pressure.

► Use your chart as a working formula, i.e. set your own goals, pull on your personal strengths to achieve them, keep problems specific and identify how they affect your goals. List development skills that you can use and call on to achieve your goals and, finally, constantly remind yourself of your achievements.

CHAPTER FOURTEEN

Friends and Social Life

WOULD YOU WANT to change your friends? I don't mean change them for new ones but change some of their character traits. Perhaps you like them exactly the way they are. If so, they might feel exactly the same way about you. Remember how I stated earlier that friends often have a vested interest in keeping you where you are?

The theme of this chapter is:

► Why some friends have a vested interest in keeping you where you are.

► Techniques for coaching your friends.

► Recognising friends who can coach you.

► Do you have to leave some friends behind in order to make the changes you desire?

► What does your social life say about you?

► Have you got the social life you desire? How can you get it?

Friendships are often based on where you are at a specific moment in your life. So if you were to meet a friend through work you may find that you have many common interests, but the overriding connection would be your mutual employment. As working hours tend to dominate a large part of people's lives, the bonds you form with work colleagues are important and valuable relationships. If your mutual connection is lost, for example if you change employment, those bonds can be broken. Once you are no longer involved in the daily interaction of that workplace, office politics become less interesting, because they no longer affect you. For the friend who remains in your previous workplace, there is no longer the same impetus to keep you up to date with the peculiarities of office life. As a result, the friendship no longer offers the same payback it once did.

▪ Vested Interests

When a friend has a vested interest in keeping you where you are it may not be as sinister as it sounds. Indeed, many friendships depend on the playing out of familiar roles such as work relationships. When those roles change, the basis of the relationship changes. You may be offering something different, which is not readily accepted by some. Equally, what they have to offer you can become less appealing. Some friends will not be able to embrace the new you, not because they want to stand in the way of your progress, but because you've become a bit of a stranger to them. And, while you haven't undergone a major personality transplant, there will be notable changes.

You could have a friend who always used to unload all their problems on you. And whereas in the past you may have merely listened and empathised, after having read this book you might get a little impatient with that process, and start wanting to ask them a few coaching questions instead, such as 'How could you turn the situation around?' or 'Have you thought about any solutions?' Since you are now dealing with your own problems in a new way and no longer staying stuck with them, it's only natural to pass on things that have worked for you. When you see the difference coaching makes to your own life your thought process changes as does the feedback you give. Who better to help than a friend? And the best way to absorb any technique fully is by teaching it to others.

Because coaching is a way of life to me, I would find it impossible to give friends the feedback I once gave them. I don't, of course, wear my coach's hat every time I'm with friends: you have to behave appropriately for each situation, and sometimes friends just want a sounding board and not a few of my forms under their noses. If a friend simply wants you to listen and be supportive, you can still do that. But, like me, you will find it harder and harder to give negative feedback. When you think positively, you will see a situation in a more positive light, even when it's relayed to you negatively. You are working on a new programme now which will affect the way you think, act and communicate. If you stay on your programme you will communicate positively about other people and yourself.

When I was going through a very difficult time with my previous company, I found that I attracted a whole set of new friends. At the time they seemed very supportive of my dilemma and I took them on face value without ever questioning their friendship. After I had made the decision to change my life, I soon realised that certain friends disappeared almost overnight. Who knows, maybe I was less interesting to them when I no longer seemed distraught and lost. Since that time I've coined a little phrase, 'the crisis hunters'. It occurred to me that certain people seem to appear as if from nowhere when there is a crisis. (Job in the Bible would have made a similar observation about his comforters.) They're not there to solve the crisis or to help you, merely to eavesdrop on your life as if they were watching a soap opera on television. Of course when that soap is your life, having a few spectators around doesn't help you.

Now, you would think that friends would want to be around the new, positive you, wouldn't you? In my own experience and that of many clients it's not the case. Some of your friends will, but not all. I'm telling you this because at the time it can be confusing and upsetting: why would those who profess friendship abandon you when you decide to get your life in order? I had always been quick to preach the benefits of moving on in life and not allowing other people's actions to detract from my own life's mission. Making the decision to change my life was certainly my salvation and if it meant leaving certain people behind, well, so be it.

You might say that I discovered who my real friends were. But it's not necessary to judge others too harshly. It's not like we're victims of a premeditated and personal attack, at least not most of the time. More often than not these people are more caught up in their own lives and what's relevant to them at the time. Perhaps observing someone in a crisis helps them to feel better about their own situation.

My own theory is that, at times in your life, you can act like a magnet to certain people. For whatever reason (and I suggest you don't waste time trying to work it out) you are offering the feedback or scenario that is attractive to them. Once you change what's on offer the new offer is less appealing to them. You may be asking whether or not they were really friends in the first place. However, past experiences have a great way of showing you both sides of the coin.

To give you an example, there may have been a time in your own life when you were stuck in a negative cycle and a friend tried to pull you out of it. At the time you didn't want to listen to what they had to say because you wanted them to agree that your situation was as bad as you were presenting it. Perhaps without even making a conscious decision you found yourself enjoying their company less or avoiding it completely. You may have sought the company of friends who you felt understood your dilemma and had similar problems. When you're stuck in a negative cycle it feels comfortable having support even when it's your negativity that's being supported. Once you decide to break that mould and move forward you will see some friends in a different light, just as they will see you in a different light in their turn. So it's not just a case of some friends finding you less appealing: you may find yourself less attracted to them.

Some useful coaching questions to ask yourself are:

▶ Which friendships do I believe are delaying my progress?

▶ Am I cultivating new friendships?

▶ Am I holding on to redundant friendships?

▶ Do I feel good about myself in the company of friends?

By now, you should be ready to work through the following exercise.

EXERCISE

▶ List the people you consider to be your friends.

▶ List the qualities you admire and associate with them.

► What do they offer?

► What do you offer?

► How much time would you like to spend with them?

► How important is it to maintain their friendship?

Using no more than three sentences, define the basis of your friendship. To help you answer those questions use the following list. Is your friendship based on: support, understanding, sharing, empathy or having fun?

Going through your list of friends, explore those friendships in more detail. Do you have any one-sided friendships? For example, do you have conversations that focus on one person's problems, triumphs, opinions and tastes exclusively? It will help you to recall how you feel most of the time when you are with a particular friend.

▪ Sing a Rainbow

The dynamics of your friendships are very varied. I remember having a conversation with singer/songwriter Lynsey de Paul, who is a good friend of mine. Lynsey told me that friends are like colours of the rainbow to her, each one representing a different colour. I thought that was a fascinating analogy because she didn't expect one friend to be all the colours; they each had something unique to offer. Some friends had more than one colour to offer while others had just the one, but they all warranted a space in her life. I think that Lynsey's interpretation of friendship makes a wonderful visualisation technique. If you see friends as colours of the rainbow you have the flexibility to allow for colour changes. The only time the friendship comes into question is when they move into the grey area.

Using the colours of the rainbow – just to remind you, they're red, orange, yellow, green, blue, indigo and violet – I'd like you to write a few sentences next to each colour, saying what it means to you. So, for example, red could represent a vivacious, fun-loving friend, whereas blue, which is a cool colour, could be a less close friend. Use your own interpretation for each colour and don't be scared of giving each one individual character traits. Once you have done that, start to place the names of friends next to a particular colour.

Like Lynsey, you may find some friends have more than one colour. If you are left with any friends that don't fit into your spectrum, these are probably your grey areas and the friendship may be redundant for the time being anyway. When you think about friends from now on you can visualise your colour spectrum and see where they fit into it. Perhaps on occasions you have expected too much from a friend and have wanted them to be all the colours. (Remember the old saying about seeing someone in their true colours?) Well I'm not convinced you only have one colour. I think we are all different things to different people and, at times, different things to the same people. Why not let your friends have a few colours? After all, just as you move through various phases, so do your friends.

You may have good reason to discontinue a particular friendship, but that's not to say you have to close the door completely or be left with regrets. Staying positive means focusing on what was good and if you reach a point when it's no longer good, you can still move on with positive memories. You don't know what the future holds and I'm sure you have already experienced friends moving in and out of your life at different times.

▪ Coaching with Friends

As I said earlier, it's only natural for you to want to help a friend. When you use techniques that move you forward, who better to share them with than friends. At times this will happen without you even realising it because you may be moving forward with a positive attitude and be much more inclined to give positive feedback. Along the way you will start to identify friends who are good coaches and support your progress. Why not share this book with a friend? That way you can both help each other and offer support. If you start to slip back, encourage a friend to remind you about your goals and, to stay positive, do the same for them. You may find it helps to sit down with a friend on a weekly basis and review your progress. To do this effectively, allocate a time slot, so that for at least half-an-hour one of you acts as coach and the other as client. That way you can both give each other your full attention. This works better than two individuals trying to discuss their charts at the same time.

▪ Social Life

How good is your social life? Does it reflect you as a person? Before we start setting goals, let's reflect on what is meant by a social life and how you can enjoy it to the full.

I bet you know someone who is never home – maybe it's you. Either way you know the sort of person I mean who is always busy and has lots to do in their spare time. Life might be a round of end-less parties, sporting activities and social gatherings. Of course your social life doesn't have to be so packed in order to be good. Some individuals keep themselves endlessly busy because they hate spending time in their own company. That's hardly a desir-able state, is it? Part of the quality time you allocate yourself should involve time alone. Time alone is important; it allows you to reflect and recharge and get your own thoughts in order with-out having the constant input of others. It's one thing to live life to the full, but quite another to cram your day so full that you leave no time to contemplate whether or not it's enjoyable.

I remember attending a talk given by a well-known and highly successful entrepreneur. I was in no doubt, as I listened to her, that for the past twenty years hers had been an action-packed life. What was interesting, though, was that as this person relayed a list of business achievements and glamorous social settings, there was no indication as to whether she had actually enjoyed any of them. She just flung out events at us like catalogue entries. A woman in the audience must have shared my attitude because when they invited questions at the end of the talk she asked, 'Where were you "at" as a person ten years ago?' The speaker looked startled and repeated, 'Ten years ago, ten years ago?' 'Yes,' continued the woman, 'were you happy with your life and enjoying it?' Obvi-ously being asked to recall exactly where you were 'at' ten years ago requires a few moments of reflection. But you couldn't help being left with the impression that the speaker had never contemplated the enjoyment factor. Despite the fact that she was able to recall detailed chronological events, there was no emotional recall. In fact she finally answered the question by saying, 'I was very busy and going at such a pace I didn't really have time to stop and think.' That answered a lot of other questions I had about her, too.

Can you imagine going through life at such a pace that twenty years of your life slip by and you never stopped to contemplate if you were doing something that made you happy? You can see why I believe that no matter how great the goals you achieve it means little without personal satisfaction. So even if you have an action-packed social life it will only benefit you if you are actually enjoying it. And of course you have to take the time to enjoy it. I call it those 'pinch yourself moments', which is a metaphor for a mental tweak when you say this is what I'm doing right now and am I enjoying it? It's so easy to keep running mentally and physically to the next event. I have a friend who never turns down an invitation, just in case she misses something. The biggest risk is that you could miss what you are doing right now.

When you plan your social life the emphasis has to be on quality time. Too often the focus can be on trying to look like you are having fun. You can get caught up with being at all the 'right' social gatherings or mixing with the 'in' crowd. Believe me, having done my own stint of the social circuit, it's not always much fun and I'm a lot more selective these days, preferring the company of interesting people as opposed to ones who are more concerned about impressing. Your social life should be reflective of you. This means reflective of the sort of person you really are and not trying to fit into other people's perceptions.

EXERCISE

Make a list of the sort of activities you like to do socially. Next to each one, state how much time you have to do it and how much time you would ideally like to have. Next to that list, make a list of the things you don't like to do socially but are involved in doing. So, for example, there may be family social gatherings, social gatherings with a partner, social functions through work. Separating out the two you can see how much time you actually spend on things you enjoy. There are less enjoyable social events that you will not necessarily be obliged to do but may agree to. Going along with them should not pose too much of a problem if you have a healthy balance of things you like to do.

In my experience very few individuals strike a good balance. Many of my clients have very busy lives, yet here are some of the common goals from their forms.

▶ Spend more time with friends

▶ Catch up with old friends

▶ Have more fun

▶ Go to the theatre/cinema more often

▶ Visit museums/art exhibitions

▶ Have more weekends away

▶ Take a holiday

Social life, like all the other areas of your life chart, requires time and if you don't monitor your time it's soon taken up doing things you'd rather not be doing. So obviously you have to plan for a social life and make a commitment to it. How often have you got together with a group of friends and said, 'We must do this more often', and yet you slip back into the old pattern with months elapsing before your next reunion? And yet this is probably something you enjoy. So, why don't you do it more often? Well, chances are you get busy with something else, life gets in the way and your social life takes second, or even third place. You may have got into a rut and in the habit of not having a social life, or perhaps there was a gradual decline. Many couples fall into this trap. At the beginning of a relationship you want to spend every available minute together and before you know it, even going out seems too much effort. There's no problem not going out if you can honestly say you are having real quality time at home. However, when your social life is in a rut, you're not enjoying quality time, especially if you are filling the space staring at a television.

Once you're in a rut you really need a kick-start to get back in the swing of things. If you find yourself turning down the majority of invitations to socialise, chances are you're in a rut. The best way out of it is to bite the bullet and force yourself to make the effort. Once you do you'll be glad you did, even if it takes a few outings before you relax and start enjoying yourself.

▪ Friends and Social Life Form

Now it's time to think about the friendships you want and the sort of social life you desire. Because this form combines both you should have plenty of goals to put in. Here are some examples.

Goals
- Increase my circle of friends
- See my friends more often
- Have more dinner parties
- Plan more social get-togethers
- Take part in a group activity/hobby
- Join in more community events
- Accept more invitations
- Throw the best parties in town

Personal strengths
- I like my friends
- I value the importance of my social life
- I'm determined to have a social life I enjoy
- I'm a very good party host
- I'm fun to be around
- I'm a loyal friend

Immediate challenges/blocks/problems
- I don't have many friends
- Most of my friends are married with children so I don't get to see much of them
- My friends aren't supportive enough
- I always end up with a hangover when I go out with friends
- My partner never wants to go out

- My children are too demanding so I have no time for a social life
- I don't have time for a social life
- I work long hours

Did some of those strike you as odd? I've deliberately dropped a few clangers in the above list, because I know by now you'll be able to spot them. Of course, they were the ones in which you're blaming other people. This is your life and your problem, so if you want to find a solution be careful how you define it.

Development skills
- Take up a new hobby
- Join a club
- Make new friends
- Talk more openly to friends
- Learn to cook so I can throw dinner parties
- Plan my social life in advance
- Telephone my friends more often
- Be there for my friends and show I'm supportive

Achievements
- I have loyal friends
- I have a good social life
- I can rely on my friends and they can rely on me
- I get asked to lots of places
- I used to have a good social life, so I know I can do it again
- I've had some great parties

▪ Improving Your Social Life

In order to have an active social life you need to know what activities are going on around you. Even in a big city, where you may be spoilt for choice, you'd be surprised how many people are lonely or have a limited social life. Of course one of the problems of city life is that it's very transient and people tend to move around a lot. You can find yourself with a different group of friends every few years. So there are plusses and minuses to every location. A quiet village may offer you less in terms of choice but there can be the benefit of long-term friendships within that community. What's really required is active participation on your part to generate a social life. Instead of waiting around to receive an invitation you could be the one to initiate it.

You can use your file to gather information on forthcoming events and places of interest to visit. It's fun planning your social calendar and it gives you something to look forward to. Certain events do require forward planning, so if you fancied a day at Ascot in June you'd have to book well in advance.

As a useful exercise, select four seasonal events for the year to look forward to, e.g. the Chelsea Flower Show, the Motor Show, Royal Ascot and a Christmas pantomime, and plan them in advance.

Once you've done that you can break the year down into months and make sure that you have at least one social treat planned each month. If you don't it's so easy for the months to slip by and you end up not doing anything you particularly enjoy. You can make an extra commitment by ordering tickets in advance. I'm sure there have been times when you had tickets to go somewhere, and perhaps got home from work that evening feeling tired and stressed. If it weren't for the fact you had tickets you would probably have stayed home, but by the end of the evening I bet you were glad you went.

▪ Conclusion

► Friends often have a vested interest in keeping you where you are. And it can work both ways.

► Be clear about what your friendships are based on.

► Use the colours of the rainbow to define your friends – they can have one colour, many colours or can change colours.

► Use this book with a friend and you can both coach each other

► Describe the sort of social life you want.

► Plan your social life in advance.

► Get information. If you want a good social life you need to know what's going on.

PART 3

Conclusion

CHAPTER FIFTEEN

The Continuing Stairway

WELL DONE! You've got through the book. But, as you will appreciate by now, coaching is an ongoing programme, a way of life in fact. And to keep making the sort of progress you have already made you have to stay with it.

You can refer to each chapter as your point of reference and, as I said at the beginning, use this book as a textbook. I am going to leave you with some final techniques to help you incorporate the seven steps into a daily programme and keep all the areas of your life in balance as you continue to progress.

Remember the scoring system we used in chapter 1? It's time to review it again.

EXERCISE

Use a scoring system from 1 to 10 (10 being the optimum score), that reflects your personal fulfilment, contentment, happiness and overall satisfaction with your present situation. Address each area briefly and select a score based on your initial feelings.

	Low									High
▪ Health	1	2	3	4	5	6	7	8	9	10
▪ Spiritual/religious life	1	2	3	4	5	6	7	8	9	10
▪ Work/career	1	2	3	4	5	6	7	8	9	10
▪ Financial	1	2	3	4	5	6	7	8	9	10

	Low									*High*
■ Personal relationships	1	2	3	4	5	6	7	8	9	10
■ Family/extended family	1	2	3	4	5	6	7	8	9	10
■ Friends/social life	1	2	3	4	5	6	7	8	9	10

To keep the seven steps in mind, look at this scoring system every day and fill in a score in your journal. The end of the day is the best time to do it. The scores may frequently change. What you need to do is review them again on a weekly basis and see how each area averages out. If there are areas that constantly fluctuate then there may be problems you are not really dealing with. So let's say your personal relationship score is going up and down like a yo-yo, or maybe it's your work and career section. You may be basing your score on the treatment you receive from a partner or boss. This may be based on their mood on a particular day, which you are subjected to. If the mood is good you have a good day and give yourself a higher score. If it's bad, your score reflects that. In reality there is a problem in that area which is stopping you achieve a balanced or consistent score. You are basing your score on where *they* are 'at' and not where *you* are 'at'. So be on the look-out for scores that fluctuate a lot.

If you score highly in areas, make sure you don't become complacent. Still continue to set goals for yourself in those areas, work on development skills and continue to update your achievements. If problems spring up in these areas, allocate a time to work through them in your mental oasis. Don't let high-scoring areas lose points by overlooking them. The aim is for all your scores to be as high as possible.

When you review your scoring system at the end of each week, spend a few minutes listing what you have done to contribute to your goals. Go through each of your forms and remind yourself of what goals you have placed in each category. Goals can and do change along the way, but in order to keep your focus on a goal it has to be at the forefront of your mind.

If you feel that you are losing points and your score is going down in any section, set yourself some specific tasks for the following week, e.g.:

- ► Go to the gym on Tuesday

- ► Call my parents on Sunday at 6 o'clock

- ► Make an appointment for the dentist on Monday morning

- ► Have a romantic dinner for two, Friday evening, with my partner

You'll find you are less likely to overlook doing something when you set specific times and days to do it.

▪ Your Year Planner

You can use an existing year planner or incorporate one of your own into your journal. Include both long- and short-term goals.

Short-term goals

Everyone has a different interpretation of what is meant by short-term goals, so we need to be a bit more specific. Let's call all your short-term goals the ones that will be achieved within a three-month period or less. Some of the goals may be larger ones that you have broken down. So, for example, if you have a long-term goal to compete in the marathon, your short-term goal for the next three months could be to do an hour-long aerobics class without getting out of breath. Once that goal is in sight you can set another short-term goal to incorporate into your fitness programme. Got the idea?

Long-term goals

To keep things simple, let's call anything over three months a long-term goal. Some people set what they call medium-term goals, but I prefer simplicity. That way you only have two goal charts to work with. In your long-term goal chart, list all the goals in order of time that you have set, e.g. :

Work/career 'In the next six months I'll get promotion; I'm on a two-year training course; in five years I'll have the necessary experience to start my own business.'

Friends/Social Life 'During the next six months I will go with friends to the cinema at least once a week and see at least twenty-four films; I will attend the school reunion at the end of the year; I will visit my best friend in Australia within the next two years.'

When you refer to your weekly list of all the ways in which you have contributed to a goal, don't overlook your long-term list. Unless you are actively contributing to it that goal remains out of reach and permanently long-term. Even if you have a five-year plan it doesn't mean you wait until the end of five years and then start to work on your goal, not unless you want it to become a ten-year plan.

A friend of mine called Nick has had a five-year plan for his career ever since he left college, which was nearly twenty years ago. He's still doing exactly the same job. It's a good job by most people's standards, but he didn't plan to be doing it for twenty years. So you could say he didn't plan to fail with his goal, he just failed to put his plan into action. Personally, I don't believe that life somehow gets in the way and stops you achieving your goals. In my book, that's just an excuse. It really is a case of not putting your plans into action. For every person I've ever met who stayed stuck and didn't realise a goal I've met equal numbers who have stayed with their goal and made it happen.

Anyone can prepare an impressive plan for their future. And I'm sure you have come across people who can talk a really good theory, but they never get round to implementing it. If you're not careful you can get too caught up in the planning. It's a trait I've observed in many people. They spend their whole life swamped in the finer detail and are ultimately distracted from the final result because they never put any plans into action. You need to get involved in the 'doing' bit so you start living your goal and not just dreaming it.

This can involve you questioning your concept of what's in store for you in the future. You see, many people set off by thinking, 'Well before I can do such and such, I need to have this or that in place'. The problem is that in the mean time, they are doing nothing to achieve the bit in the middle. Take my advice: if you are convinced that there is a good reason for not implementing a goal immediately, make sure you are still contributing to that goal.

Opportunities have to be seized and sometimes you have to jiggle with the sequence of events to make them happen. So, if you'll excuse me, I'd like to tell one final story, this time about me.

When I was first asked to write a book on coaching I was immediately excited about doing it. My first thoughts were that here was the perfect opportunity to share something that had changed my life for the better. Although I refer clients to other coaching organisations when my own books are full, I still work alone. I approve the techniques and methods used by those I refer to, otherwise I wouldn't put clients on to them. But at the end of the day I'm sure we all have our own unique message and way of working. And the best way for you to judge the effectiveness is if it works for you. My methods worked for me and I am lucky enough to have the feedback from my clients when it works for them. Their case histories made this book possible and when many of them agreed to be included I knew this was the right thing to do.

Life has a wonderful way of surprising you. However far you think you have come there is always a new challenge on the horizon. This book was a new challenge for me because I had never written a book before. I had looked at several coaching manuals and thought: I could do better than that, but actually writing a book required me to stop criticising and actually put my thoughts down on paper. I can tell you, hand on heart, it was the hardest thing, career-wise, I've ever done in my life to date. It required a level of discipline that I've never previously experienced. A few years ago, as I've said earlier, I resigned from my own company. I loved that company with a passion, and yet to a certain extent my previous business had become too easy for me and there was no element of risk. On reflection it would have been easy to stay with that comfort factor had a dispute not thrown a spanner in the works. But when I used the techniques I have shared with you to revisit the past, the biggest fear for me was leaving that comfort zone and facing a new challenge.

Each challenge you face takes place on a personal level. There is no universal scale of success, only your own levels of success. Every time it hurts, you know you are pushing yourself beyond your own boundaries. You will enjoy it in the process, believe me: that hill is worth climbing.

There is something phenomenally powerful about writing out

your goals. While I may share with you my own theories on the 'Why', I have no conclusive answer as to 'What it is'. What I can tell you is that even for the converted like me, the speed at which things can happen is breathtaking. In January 1998 I wrote down the goal to write this book. Within three months I had my first offer from a publisher. A month later I had a second offer, which was the one I accepted. There were several other goals on my list, all of which at the time of writing have been realised or are in the process of being realised. Was I active in realising them? You bet I was. Was it scary? You bet it was.

I faced my own monsters. While I could talk a good theory to my clients, my lack of education suddenly proved very limiting when it came to writing them down. Thank God for development skills, because what you lack now you can gain at some later date. And I've got myself down to go on a creative writing course in the very near future.

So, as you can see, even when you believe what you are doing is right and you feel passionate about it, as I do about my work, you still have to overcome your own personal fears. What makes the difference is holding on to that strength of feeling, because if you hold on to it you'll overcome your fears, and passion will be your driving force. And the best way to stop fear diluting your passion is by separating out the two. Fear is like a little splinter that gets under your skin and if you don't get it out it will start an infection and work its way into your whole system. So the minute you feel the prickly effects of those dreaded splinters, you must make a conscious effort to root them out.

To achieve certain goals, you may be faced with practical limitations or feel that you don't have enough talent to be successful in that area. However it's not the most talented individuals who make it, it's the most determined ones. And that's my overriding message to you in this book. Your goals are achievable: all it takes is for you to believe it and you'll find a way to make them happen. The only thing that can hold you back or limit you from realising your full potential is fear, so you have to learn to stop it infecting your passion. Use it to your advantage. If fear is telling you that you can't do something, go out and prove it wrong. Fill in your missing blanks. There is no real logic to your fear or accurate point of reference. Even if things didn't work out in the past you are still faced with a new scenario that allows you to change the running order. It really is up to you. Once you start to use your brain to work out some tactical manoeuvres you'll get to wherever it is you want to go.

Some challenges and goals will feel uphill every step of the way. That's fine, because you are doing your groundwork in the process. There will be some development skills that seem to come amazingly easily. Others you will have to be patient about, but trust yourself: you will acquire them along the way. What's really important is the formula you are subscribing to. And just to remind you, here it is:

► Set your goals.

► Make a commitment to achieving them.

► Meet your challenges head on.

► When the problem seems too great, break it down and find a workable solution.

► Avoid blaming other people.

► Keep your problems specific to you and see the part you play in your own life.

► You are the sideline spectator when you view a problem and the active player when you solve it.

► Be clear about what you want and why you want it. Does it fit in with your values?

► Are you making excuses for not getting what you want? Is it easier to avoid your fears than face them?

► Communicate your message. If other people can't see it, remember this is your vision, and not everyone will see it. But if they don't hear it, maybe you're not using the right language.

► Work on your goals on a daily basis, even if they are long-term goals.

And with that formula in mind, let me wish you every success with your coaching programme. I hope that the techniques you have read in this book will become an invaluable part of your everyday life.

PART 4

The Forms

HEALTH

Goals

1

2

3

Personal Strengths

1

2

3

Immediate Challenges/Blocks/Problems

1

2

3

Development Skills

1

2

3

Achievements

1

2

3

SPIRITUAL

Goals

1

2

3

Personal Strengths

1

2

3

Immediate Challenges/Blocks/Problems

1

2

3

Development Skills

1

2

3

Achievements

1

2

3

WORK

Goals

1

2

3

Personal Strengths

1

2

3

Immediate Challenges/Blocks/Problems

1

2

3

Development Skills

1

2

3

Achievements

1

2

3

FINANCES

Goals

1

2

3

Personal Strengths

1

2

3

Immediate Challenges/Blocks/Problems

1

2

3

Development Skills

1

2

3

Achievements

1

2

3

PERSONAL RELATIONSHIPS

Goals

1

2

3

Personal Strengths

1

2

3

Immediate Challenges/Blocks/Problems

1

2

3

Development Skills

1

2

3

Achievements

1

2

3

FAMILY

Goals

1

2

3

Personal Strengths

1

2

3

Immediate Challenges/Blocks/Problems

1

2

3

Development Skills

1

2

3

Achievements

1

2

3

FRIENDS AND SOCIAL LIFE

Goals

1

2

3

Personal Strengths

1

2

3

Immediate Challenges/Blocks/Problems

1

2

3

Development Skills

1

2

3

Achievements

1

2

3

Further Reading

Be Your Own Best Friend, Louis Proto, Piatkus (1994)

Calm at Work, Paul Wilson, Penguin (1997)

Feel the Fear and Do it Anyway, Susan Jeffers, HarperCollins (1992)

Good Relationship Guide, Dr Maryon Tysoe, Piatkus (1998)

Heart Thoughts, Louise L. Hay, Eden Grove Editions (1991)

Making Friends: A Guide to Getting Along with People, Andrew Matthews, Media Masters (1990)

Mind Detox, Deborah Marshall-Warren, Thorsons (1998)

Mind Power, Christian Godefroy and D. R. Steevens, Piatkus (1998)

The Optimum Nutrition Bible, Patrick Holford, Piatkus (1997)

Organise Yourself, Ronnie Eisenberg and Kate Kelly, Piatkus (1997)

Perfect Communications, Andrew Leigh and Michael Maynard, Arrow Business Books (1994)

Perfect Decisions, Andrew Leigh, Century Business Books (1993)

Perfect Health, Deepak Chopra, Bantam Books (1990)

The Psychology of Personal Constructs, George Kelly, W. W. Norton & Co (1963)

The Seven Habits of Highly Effective Families, Stephen R. Covey, Franklin Covey (1997)

The Seven Spiritual Laws of Success, Deepak Chopra, Bantam Books (1996)

Success Through a Positive Mental Attitude, Napoleon Hill and W. Clement Stone, Pocket Books (1992)

The Tao of Coaching, Max Landsberg, HarperCollins (1996)

Teach Yourself to Think, Edward de Bono, Penguin (1996)

You Can't Afford the Luxury of a Negative Thought, John Rogers and Peter McWilliams, Prelude Press (1995)

Index